Praise for *The Inner Voice of Trading*

"Michael Martin has written an insightful book for both the expert and novice. His writing style is enjoyable, and the content is unforgettable."

—Anthony Scaramucci, Founder, SkyBridge Capital, and Author of *Goodbye Gordon Gekko*

"I live by Michael Martin's words. The first chapter of my investing book was titled 'Turn Off the TV.' Now, with the social web, finding strategy mentors and learning faster are all possible. Trading is a skill you can learn, and Martin's book is a great read for any trader."

—Howard Lindzon, Founder, StockTwits

"In *The Inner Voice of Trading*, Michael Martin recounts his own quest to become a successful trader, illuminating his journey with engaging trading episodes. Join Martin at his trading desk as he provides important insights into the art and science of balancing thoughts and feelings—and catching the big one."

—Ed Seykota

"Some people trade and either don't or can't teach; some people teach and have never traded; Michael Martin can teach extremely well and is an experienced trader. This rare combo is a necessity to those who want to succeed in the markets. Read and learn!"

—Victor Sperandeo, Founder, Alpha Financial Technologies, LLC

"*The Inner Voice of Trading* provides insights that may help both discretionary and systematic traders adhere to their extensively researched and tested trading programs and be better insulated from their occasional emotional (fear, greed, pride, and so on) temptations to deviate into uncharted waters."

—Bill Dunn, DUNN Capital Management

"Michael Martin provides a toolbox to fortify the most important aspect of successful trading: the six inches between your ears. With fresh insights from many of the market's greatest traders, *The Inner Voice of Trading* will put you on the path to improving your profits and losses."

—John Del Vecchio, Portfolio Manager, AdvisorShares Active Bear ETF

"Too many new and developing traders move from strategy to strategy in the hope of improving their under performance. In *The Inner Voice of Trading*, Michael Martin helps us understand how we first must work on ourselves before we can become the trader we want to be. Find a place in your trading library for this latest gift to the trading community."

—Mike Bellafiore, Partner, SMB Capital, and Author of *One Good Trade*

The Inner Voice of Trading

The Inner Voice of Trading

Eliminate the Noise, and Profit from the Strategies That Are Right for You

Michael Martin

Vice President, Publisher: Tim Moore
Associate Publisher and Director of Marketing: Amy Neidlinger
Executive Editor: Jim Boyd
Development Editor: Russ Hall
Senior Marketing Manager: Julie Phifer
Assistant Marketing Manager: Megan Graue
Cover Designer: Alan Clements
Managing Editor: Kristy Hart
Project Editors: Jess DeGabriele and Jovana San Nicolas-Shirley
Copy Editor: Krista Hansing Editorial Services, Inc.
Proofreader: Water Crest Publishing, Inc.
Senior Indexer: Cheryl Lenser
Senior Compositor: Gloria Schurick
Manufacturing Buyer: Dan Uhrig

Publishing as FT Press
Upper Saddle River, New Jersey 07458

Printed in the United States of America

First Printing September 2011

ISBN-10: 0-13-261625-4
ISBN-13: 978-0-13-261625-6

Pearson Education LTD.
Pearson Education Australia PTY, Limited.
Pearson Education Singapore, Pte. Ltd.
Pearson Education North Asia, Ltd.
Pearson Education Canada, Ltd.
Pearson Educatión de Mexico, S.A. de C.V.
Pearson Education—Japan
Pearson Education Malaysia, Pte. Ltd.

Library of Congress-in-Publication Data:

Martin, Michael R. (Michael Robert), 1966-

The inner voice of trading : eliminate the noise, and profit from the system and strategies that are right for you / Michael R. Martin.
p. cm.
ISBN-13: 978-0-13-261625-6 (hardcover : alk. paper)
ISBN-10: 0-13-261625-4 (hardcover : alk. paper)
1. Floor traders (Finance)—United States—Psychology. 2. Futures market—United States—Psychological aspects. 3. Financial futures—United States—Psychological aspects. 4. Investments—Psychological aspects. I. Title.
HG4621.M38 2011
332.64'5—dc23

2011023680

Dedicated to my parents,
Robert J. Martin and
Anne M. Martin

Table of Contents

Foreword

Michael Martin's book, *The Inner Voice of Trading*, provides important insights about the art and science of balancing thoughts and feelings in trading.

Traders tell wonderful stories about making phenomenal profits by being in the zone, at one with the markets, living in the moment of now. From there, trading seems effortless. The trick, then, is to stay in the now. If you get impatient or greedy or fearful, you can break the spell and wind up back in the past and future. Fighting your feelings can be anathema to staying in the moment, hence to trading profitably.

In *The Inner Voice of Trading*, Martin extends the literature on the art and science of staying clear and maintaining mental and emotional balance. He uses examples from his own trading and others' to illustrate his points—particularly the importance of timely surrender.

Traders know the essential principles of trading: ride your winners; cut your losers; manage your risk; use stops; stick to your system and ignore the news. These principles work well in trading and in life in general—when you follow them consistently. Many people, however, find that following rules is not always a whole lot of fun.

Living a principle-centric life takes character—lots of it. Buying highs, selling lows, and collecting seemingly endless strings of whipsaws may bring up unbearably uncomfortable feelings. Martin deals directly with the important character-success connection and illustrates the topic by wrapping it in a series of engaging trading episodes.

One of the pleasures of mentoring traders through my Trading Tribe® is that I get to meet, interact with, and share experiences with bright and willing people—and to watch them grow and prosper. And that brings me to one Mr. Michael Martin who, many moons ago, joins my Tribe.

At first I see an east-coast, street-wise hyper-mensch, a cross between a crusty old cabbie and a stand-up comic. As the group evolves, I witness his emergence as a brother who comes to feel deeply and laugh and wince and cry and grieve along with the rest of us as we all struggle with the personal calculus of our careers and intimate relationships.

Over the course of our association I have the privilege of witnessing a softening of Michael—as he becomes more porous, stronger, and more available to share his gifts with others. Reading between the lines of *Inner Voice*, I feel that Michael is still very much a man of the path and that he is now coming into his own as a generous teacher, mentor, and writer. I see him as a big inspiration for the new crop.

It is my honor to accept Michael Martin's invitation to pen this forward to his book. I congratulate him for writing it—and you for reading it.

Ed Seykota

Austin, Texas

Acknowledgments

Michael Marcus, Ed Seykota, Jorgen Christiansson, Aaron Brown, Peter Borish, Bill Dunn, Erich Schiffmann, Tom Basso, BKS Iyengar, Linda Raschke, Victor Sperandeo, Mike Bellafiore, Steve Spencer, Helmut Weymar, Larry Shover, John Del Vecchio, Willow Bay, Maria Russo, Richard Sandor, Carole Brookins.

Thank Yous

Michael J. Rice, Eleanor Johnson, Harris Sperling, Tony "Fat Tony" Tardino, Pia Varma, Rich Blake, JJF, Manish Jain, Scott Kaminski, Yasmine Ryckebusch, Erin FitzPatrick, Liz, Gabrielle and Mark LaMura, Stacy-Marie Ishmael, Maryanne Martin, Luc Eamon Martin, Loyal Seamus Martin, TJ O'Connor, Kieran Gaine, Shawn Patt, Bryan Kenny and Monica Sarang, James Robert Anthony Durfey, Douglas Mancino, Peter and Heather Felix, Gerard Colagrossi, Mugsy, Melissa Moore and Jerry Toepke, Carey Doss, Mike Holwick, Joanna "J-Go" Grzeskowiak, Andrew Homsi, Rich Burnes, Margaret Rees, Amy Geffen, Maryann Kelly, Alex Lapostol, Calvin Slater, Richard Hughes, Wendy and JJ Mueller, Bud Ardell, Susan Bursk, Karim Cherif, John Christesen, Joseph Hankin, Bert Liberi, Jr., James Little, Scott McIntosh, Melissa Bell and Leo Schmidt, Ana LaDou, Simon and Monna Mainwaring, Nelly Nyambi, Lenny Mo.

As far as the publishing of this book is concerned, I owe a special thank you to my Executive Editor Jim Boyd who believed in the vision for this book from the get-go. Jim introduced me to Russ Hall as well as uber-author Michael Thomsett who were instrumental for their keen insight and suggestions. I am grateful for the staggering amount of time that Jim, Russ, and Michael spent reviewing the evolving manuscript.

About the Author

Michael Martin has been a successful trader for over 20 years. He's been teaching for the last 13 of those years through UCLA Extension and the New York Society of Security Analysts (NYSSA), a member society of the CFA Institute. During that time, he also served as Associate Editor at *Trader Monthly*. He was born and raised in New York and now lives in Los Angeles.

He contributes to *The Huffington Post*, *The Business Insider*, and his blog MartinKronicle.com. He has also been published in Barron's.

His interest in trading commodities began as a student, both in the classroom and at work. It was during a random work-study program that he got introduced to creating seasonal models for Heating Oil and Natural Gas for a large hedger using Lotus 123.

That led to working on Wall Street and trading commodity accounts. The commissions were gigantic, but he figured he could earn several times more by earning an incentive fee. After only 3 years at a brokerage firm, he started his own company.

After moving to Los Angeles from Manhattan, he started his own CTA and also began teaching. Around that time he joined the Incline Village Trading Tribe and flew from Los Angeles to Lake Tahoe for meetings. He also formed the Trading Tribe in Los Angeles, for which he was Chief. Coincidence or not, he was ranked #1 by AutumnGold around that time.

His trading courses are available online and can be found at MartinKronicle.com.

Chapter 1

Introduction

Like many traders, I became very interested in trading professionally after I read Jack D. Schwager's book *Market Wizards,* a collection of interviews that he'd conducted with many successful traders and money managers at the time, such as Jim Rogers, Paul Tudor Jones, and Michael Marcus. Luckily for me, I was able to get to know and study with many of the traders interviewed. A few of them, such as Ed Seykota, became mentors and friends who had a profound impact on my psychological outlook while trading.

A lot of traders love the Seykota chapter in *Market Wizards* and can quote what might be his most famous line: "Win or lose, everyone gets what they want from the market." To this day, that line hits failing and mediocre traders right in their most vulnerable spot: If a trader is losing consistently, it is by design—it is the trader's goal. For Seykota and his students, intentions equal results.

> "The goal for the trader is to develop a system with which he is compatible"—that is, a harmony between a trader's emotional constitution and trading technique.

However, I think that the most revealing thought in the chapter was another of Seykota's quotes: "The goal for the trader is to develop a system with which he is compatible"—that is, a harmony between a trader's emotional constitution and trading technique. In this case, a system is a set of rules for trading: what to buy, how much of it to own, when to get in, and when to get out, either to take a loss or to collect profits. These rules are intellectual in nature—at least, that's how they look from the outside.

Lurking below the surface are the emotional buttons they push when the trader employs them. The intellectual aspect of trading rules are what most aspiring traders reach for while learning the craft because they've had that approach ingrained in them since kindergarten. Unfortunately, most aspiring traders find out far too late that the act of trading is 20% intellectual and 80% psychological. I hope to change that with this book.

When Seykota was being interviewed, he was not speaking about rules "that [the trader] can understand intellectually or technically"—he wasn't offering a "how to trade" proposition. He instead referred to rules "with which [the trader] is compatible," an emotional and self-awareness proposition. Compatibility equals harmony.

Incompatibility between trader and system is the single greatest reason most traders don't succeed, regardless of trading style. They have no emotional connection to their trading rules and methodology. They know trading rules from a technical and intellectual standpoint, but not from a psychological or self-awareness one. Not all of this is their fault, though: Our educational system generally is not concerned with how its students feel about anything—there's no room for it. This rote, mechanical model sets up the trader for failure before he knows that he wants to be a trader. Admittedly, it can be challenging to know who to turn to for this type of awakening. In unfortunate cases, the trader is not self-aware but continues to seek the answers. Ironically, these answers to successful trading are found within the trader's own mind.

Incompatibility between trader and system is the single greatest reason most traders don't succeed, regardless of trading style. They have no emotional connection to their trading rules and methodology. They know trading rules from a technical and intellectual standpoint, but not from a psychological or self-awareness one.

To trade successfully, your intellect and psychology must be joined at the hip. Like spouses in a marriage, both intellect and self-awareness evolve. If the self-aware spouse checks out, maintaining a lasting marriage is difficult. The situation puts stress on both spouses. If one partner needs time "to figure out who he is," a trial separation is best, to keep the trader from vaporizing the cash. A trader without self-awareness in trading is like a pilot trying to fly a plane with no navigator.

Trading rules are provocative and evocative, pushing and pulling a trader emotionally. "Should I get in at this price?" "Should I buy some of this stock?" "Should I get out here and take a loss, or should I wait for it to come back?" For me, these are not intellectual questions—they are emotional. What the trader is feeling at the time evokes the question. Think about what the trader is conveying emotionally, because it's rarely about the money.

> Question: "Should I get in at this price? Is now a good time to buy?"
>
> Emotional translation: "I have no idea what I'm doing, but I'm going to do it anyway."
>
> Question: "Should I buy some of this stock?"
>
> Emotional translation: "I want in on the action. Just tell me what to do, and I'll do it—but make it quick. Having so much cash is painful."

According to Jason Zweig,[1] having the potential for gains is more addictive than earning the gains themselves.

> Question: "Should I take the loss now, or wait for it to come back?"
>
> Emotional translation: "What will everyone think? I have an MBA, and all my self-esteem is invested in how smart I think I am. I am not willing to risk this. This is who I am. If I wait, I'm technically not wrong. I can defer my incorrectness and maintain my self-esteem today."

Traders are human beings first, so it follows that everything we do is part of our overall tendency to seek pleasure and avoid pain. Both are omnipresent for traders and investors alike. In each of these hypothetical questions, clearly more is being conveyed than the "how to" part of trading. Frankly, the "how to" is the easy part. When the self-awareness part betrays the "how to" part because traders don't have the skill to feel emotions and understand what they are saying, only trouble can come from it. If you get into this situation, along with all the colorful emotional knots you'll feel in your body, you'll have a black-and-white version in your profit and loss statement.

A trader doesn't need another person to ask these questions, nor to answer them. For traders who lack harmony between technique and self-awareness, the voice they hear comes from the most antagonistic person in their life: "You should have become a doctor! I told you that this trading nonsense is legalized gambling." However, once they achieve a harmony between technical rules and self-awareness, they discover an inner calm and a sense of confidence. When this occurs, they hold conversations with what I call their *inner voice*. This is the one voice that the "market wizards" developed and learned to listen to exclusively.

For traders who lack harmony between technique and self-awareness, the voice they hear comes from the most antagonistic person in their life.

The heart and soul of this book examines trading decisions from an emotional standpoint and helps you gain insight into your behavior. In the process, you will evolve from listening to the cacophony of conformist and conventional wisdom, to speaking with and listening to your *inner voice*. The journey involves getting to know yourself and increasing your level of self-awareness. How much you learn about yourself is limited only by which feelings you are *not* willing to feel.

The longer you attended school, the more ingrained the "how to" approach is in your learning model and your "accuracy model" of keeping score. You may be used to thinking along these lines: "If I get 90+% of the questions correct, I'll get an A on the exam. If I do that several times in a row, I'll get an A for the class." Accuracy and correctness become the goals. Nowhere is the concept of self-awareness addressed verbally or literally, but it is expressed in others' behavior at home and in your social circle, based on how others act with you and around you.

> The heart and soul of this book examines trading decisions from an emotional standpoint and helps you gain insight into your behavior.

This situation works in trading as well. Before you became a trader, you may have gone to college for your MBA. You may have opted to achieve one of the most difficult professional designations: the CFA (Chartered Financial Analyst). Your parents likely are proud of you, and you're proud of yourself—and you should be. You clearly have more education than most of your peers and most of the world. But despite all your demonstrable intelligence and wisdom, you may still have trouble executing the single most important tool in your trading arsenal: keeping your losses small. The reason is simple: Smart people don't like being wrong. You've built your whole life on living the life of success. It's more comfortable because that's what you're used to. As a trader, you'd rather stay in a losing position and wait for the market to prove your thesis correct than take one of many consistent small losses.

Social mores are hard at work, too. They create conflict between trading profitably and your tendency to desire accuracy in all your endeavors. It feels better to strive to be correct than to face defeat. In this case, the banal mantra of "Winners never quit" doesn't serve you in managing risk—and that's what traders are, risk managers. Winners never quit, but quitters have more equity in their accounts when they admit defeat and return tomorrow with a fresh start and a clear head. They are not distracted by having to wait on their emotional front porches for some losing position to come home profitably.

It's not that you don't get it, but you're not emotionally able to reconcile how smart you are with the emotional-based behavior that you think you must execute in the trading profession if you want to compete. It's not about making gains alone (a game of pure accuracy)—it's about consistently making less frequent gains that are several times the size of the losses (a game of mathematical expectation). Professional traders approach taking risks according to the concept of mathematical expectation which addresses the provocative nature of traders being wrong more than 50% of the time (not accurate), yet be wildly profitable, and most importantly, emotionally placated throughout the trading process. Understanding mathematical expectation can help bridge the chasm between intellect and self-awareness. This is probably the single most important tool you have for developing your inner voice. Consider an example.

Imagine the following rates of return for five equally weighted positions in a hypothetical portfolio, Scenario A:

Position 1	+25%
Position 2	+10%
Position 3	Flat, neither gain nor loss
Position 4	–10%
Position 5	–25%

For all the hard work in putting this portfolio together, the overall return is flat. Positions 1 and 2 indicate skill or luck, and positions 4 and 5 indicate lack of skill or bad luck. But because all the positions are the same size, the overall rate of return for the portfolio is zero. Many traders further complicate matters by selling positions 1 and 2 and leaving positions 3, 4, and 5 to see if they will come back. That's the equivalent of pulling your flowers and letting your weeds bloom.

Now reconsider the same list two months later (Scenario B), with some risk management employed:

Position 1	+25%
Position 2	+10%
Position 3	Flat
Position 4	–10% (sold)
Position 5	–10% (sold)

Regardless of why positions 1 and 2 appreciated and positions 4 and 5 depreciated, they moved. In scenario B, because positions 4 and 5 were eliminated before depreciating further, the portfolio achieved an overall rate of return of +3%—and no one knows whether it was due to skill or luck. Taking losses in positions 4 and 5 involves self-discipline and surrender. These are emotional and self-awareness concerns, not intellectual ones. By employing this self-awareness and discipline in a portfolio and keeping losses small, both experts and dart-throwers perform better. After selling the losers, Portfolio B is 60% invested and has 40% in cash. Winners thrive in this environment. If this trader has an evolved inner voice, he doesn't waste energy wondering about the losing positions. He thinks clearly and focuses on taking the next steps, adding to the winners, and taking on new positions. His portfolio is in harmony with his head. His positions and his portfolio are compatible with his goals. They are making money. As a trader, your gains will look like gains in your overall profit and loss statement when you keep your losses small.

In addition, these positions don't care what you think about them. Imagine that position 4 or 5 was Apple stock, and perhaps you have an emotional attachment to the security because of your fondness for the company's products or its CEO. Apple is not a person with feelings, and it doesn't have a "red phone" with a direct line to Steve Jobs so that you can tell him that you own the stock because you think he is an incredible genius. Apple has no idea that you even own its stock in your portfolio, especially if you own it in street name. To develop your inner voice, you need to see Apple solely as a vehicle for you to capture the forces of supply and demand, regardless of the length of time you own it. The minute you become emotionally attached to a stock, you lose the rational ability to keep your losses small. You've become emotionally invested in the outcome.

If this were my portfolio, I would have also sold position 3. If a security has not moved in either direction after two months, I sell. When you purchase a security, only three things can happen: It goes up, down, or sideways. In two of the three scenarios, I am wrong. It doesn't matter whether I lost money—I am wrong. Traders refer to this type of liquidation as a "time stop," offsetting a position after ample time has transpired and the security has not produced any profits.

Some traders look for stocks and trading ideas to hotwire their portfolios because they see trading as a process of singling out tomorrow's headlines before they make the news. A magazine could publish just one issue per year with the headline "Keep Your Losses to a Minimum of –10% of Your Net Capital." They would go a great distance in defeating financial illiteracy, but financial literacy is not their business. They're in the business of selling magazines and keeping ad rates high. When you develop your inner voice, you can see things more clearly and laugh like I do when I see headlines such as "CMGI Is the Berkshire Hathaway of the Internet" or "10 Stocks the Pros Are Buying Now." With or without funny magazine covers, trading is a process that focuses on keeping losses small. Focus on that process, not the outcome.

> In my experience, when a new position goes against you, it usually keeps going down. Good trades start making you money right away.

The little trader in your brain may be asking, "What happens if I get out at –10% and it comes back?" Emotional translation: "What happens if I feel frustrated and look stupid at the same time?" If you're asking yourself these questions, you may be emotionally tied to the name of the company and your educational level. Furthermore, when you're first starting out, you're likely to feel one of two different things about a trade. You feel the first if you sell at a –10% loss; you feel the other if you let the position continue to bleed to –50% of its original value. You have a choice. When you listen to your inner trader, that choice is easy.

In my experience, when a new position goes against you, it usually keeps going down. Good trades start making you money right away. You can always get back in if you exit too soon. The takeaway is that you can never let a single losing trade wipe out any of your gains—they're hard enough to get in the first place. The next step is to explore your feelings about frustration or despondency and listen to what they tell you. Surrender and accept market movements, and feel a –10% move the same as you do a +25% one. By allowing yourself to feel frustration, you eliminate the feelings of despondency for the rest of your life. That's a great trade.

By allowing yourself to feel frustration, you eliminate the feelings of despondency for the rest of your life. That's a great trade.

Your feelings are the true components of your trading rules and methodology, and the technical indicators you employ are more emotional validators than technical indicators. When you've fully developed your inner voice, you'll be able to say to yourself, "To be in the trades that make it to +25%, I need to emotionally endure trades that depreciate 10%." It's like saying that you can endure getting 5% of the questions wrong on the test and still get an A for the exam and the class. The outcome you seek is to make money overall—that is the A, in this case, even if you are incorrect on your trades more than 50% of the time.

Here's how I grade my students' behavior. I tell them that the day you can tell me that your best trade was a losing one, but one by which you acted consistently in your methodology, is the day that you are on to something. The day that you tell me that your best trade lost money and that you are emotionally placated is the day that that you start behaving like a professional trader. When you can do that for three years consistently, you will have become a professional trader. Ultimately, if you want to become a professional trader, you will want to understand mathematically and emotionally that trading losses are a part of the business. Make sure they're small.

I'm not the only person to believe that real goals, deep down, have nothing to do with trading and making money, but instead center on the emotional journey that trading will involve. Different trading systems evoke different emotional responses between genders, too. Women process their feelings better, but they don't like to compete head to head. Men love to compete, but they don't like to talk about their feelings. Women can bond and make friends in the ladies' undergarments section of a department store. Men, being men, would like to make friends with women in the ladies' undergarments section. Underwear, like stocks, can evoke strong emotional responses.

If you want to get a head start on developing your inner voice, start writing down in a journal all the feelings that surface for you when reading this book or in your trading. You need to keep a journal because you have to be hypervigilant about your behavior. How do you feel you are challenged intellectually? How do you feel when someone (like me) challenges something that you've held close for ages? You will learn about yourself with this exercise, and it will benefit your trading. Timothy Ferriss, author of *The 4-Hour Body,* has kept a journal of every workout he's done since the age of 18. He's in his thirties now. What you measure, you can improve. You can use a computer for a lot of trading, but you cannot delegate all your behavior to a computer. You need insight about yourself to develop your inner voice. If you haven't begun to trade yet, that's even better. Self-knowledge and self-awareness are your most important assets as a trader, more than any technical ability. You'll have an enormous edge on the competition if you focus on developing your self-awareness and then your inner voice.

I know what the little trader in your head is saying... "But Michael, I'm dying to start trading right now. I don't have any time for keeping a journal—I'm going to miss out on all these great trades. Plus, I want to be able to call myself a trader." No one cares if you become a trader. Become a trader for yourself, not to seek attention from other people. You've heard about the moth and the flame, right? Settle down and go read *Outliers,* by Malcolm Gladwell. If you're just beginning your career, you're just starting to log the first of the 10,000 hours that Gladwell says you'll need to become an expert, so you're in no hurry. You can write in your journal, "What are my feelings when I have to be patient?" Teach me what it feels like to be you when you have to be patient. Get to know these feelings, because they are likely to resurface in other areas of your life. One of the most important things I learned from Seykota is that the feelings you don't want have as much power over you in your trading as the ones you do want. The feelings you're avoiding might be dying to become your allies. You will go to great lengths to avoid certain feelings as much as you will want to "go toward the light" to feel the ones you think you want. Make sure that light is not a bug zapper.

If you become a professional trader, you will work hard for the rest of your life. What have you had to work hard for? How have you developed character? For traders, the most important work each day is preparation for the next day. This occurs somewhere between 5 PM and 10 PM each night. How do you feel about missing the Sunday night game of the week, *60 Minutes*, and *Monday Night Football*? You can always come back to your Fantasy Football league in a few years. Has missing *Dancing with the Stars* gotten you down? Great. That feeling is in the way of you working toward your goal of becoming a trader. Write those feelings in your journal, because they are part of your emotional system.

I once read a quote from Vladimir Nabokov: "A writer is someone for whom writing is more difficult than it is for other people." I was blown away by that insight, especially since I had read some of his books. How could a writer of his stature admit something with such candor? It hit me that Nabokov had a strong inner voice. His technical ability was married by his emotional constitution. After 23 years of trading, I understand where he was coming from. If there is an analogy to this in the world of trading, a trader is someone who has let go of the emotional need to be right all the time and has learned to love taking consistent small losses the majority of the time. He does not seek validation from his trades. He doesn't need advice from others, and he enjoys a personal discipline that very few have. He has married his technical knowledge with his feelings, and the resulting inner voice is his greatest asset and ally. This book attempts to shed light on how successful traders have come to this insight and what they had to do to obtain it.

Chapter 2

Surrender

"Train yourself to let go of everything you fear to lose."
—Yoda, "Star Wars Episode III Revenge of the Sith"

A giant disconnect exists in the education of future traders. Most people who are drawn to risk management become oriented in the external "how to" aspect of trading, versus the inner aspect of emotions and psychology. This is where the trouble begins.

For traders educated in the U.S., our approach to learning is ingrained in us by our educational system. From an early age, we attend a school system that rewards us for accuracy. The teacher lectures, assigns reading material and homework, and then quizzes and tests on how much of it we've retained. Despite the banality of this process, the more we regurgitate, the higher we score. In the process, we become conditioned to adhere to the accuracy model and system of learning and reward.

The longer we remain in this reward model, the more the model becomes our way of life in everything we do. We spend 16 years in this model between kindergarten and our baccalaureate studies, so the model becomes second nature to us: We don't have to think about what we need to do to get ahead.

Accuracy and precision are rewarded. Imprecision and inexactness are not only bad, but they are considered failures—and that's where your self-esteem takes its first shot to the chin. You avoid failure at all costs, especially when it concerns the potential for public incorrectness. I think this partly explains why the analysts on financial television channels come up with reasons (read: excuses) for their recommendations not panning out. They seem to always refer to something, usually a statistical outlier, that explains why their market call failed "but would have worked out" had this outlier not occurred. It's one thing to be wrong betting on the Yankees; it's another when everyone in your office knows your errors.

If you were incorrect in school, you likely studied harder for the next exam or quiz. In other words, you put more time in and studied the "how to" part more rigorously. Of course, being able to regurgitate facts, figures, or concepts says nothing about you as a person. But not knowing them does.

Now, what if you had a professor or teacher who had a little foresight and wanted to teach you about taking smart chances in life? Say that, instead of giving you 50 true/false questions worth two points each, the instructor gave you a choice of the same 50 true/false questions, but also gave you four essay questions worth 30 points each. You could choose between the two types of exams.

Assuming that you had the same amount of time, which would you attempt to complete? If it's possible to get higher than 100% on the exam (and you could use the extra credit), would you go for the easy two-pointers when you're sure to get at least 40 of them correct, or would you go for 75% accuracy in the essays?

I encourage the students in my trader-mentoring program to take the second choice. In fact, I don't allow them to choose the first. They must make high expected value choices, even if that means getting more than half the questions incorrect or not even having enough time to get to them. In trading, most of the time you're wrong in your choices, and you have 10,000 potential securities to trade. Outlier events occur every day that escape even the largest traders. You can't live with regret. This teaches students that they will miss out regularly and may still be wildly successful.

How you trade, what you trade, and the frequency of the trades you make all come down to who you are as a person, not what you know about a specific financial instrument.

Seeking a Holy Grail in trading, based on education, is deadly. If you seek a master's degree or a professional designation like the Chartered Market Technician (CMT) or Chartered Financial Analyst (CFA), your behavioral conditioning will likely worsen, not improve. You'll come to believe that you are an expert—and you might be, from an informational perspective. But given that 60% to 80% of trading is emotional and psychological, these designations have little or no bearing on how you will do as a risk manager or trader. On top of this, although you may be entirely self-aware, you still must contend with the general level of emotional intelligence in your office. If you're lucky, you'll be rewarded for risk control and performance based on risk-adjusted returns. It's no surprise that SAC had the late great Ari Kiev on staff and that Dr. Brett Steenbarger works exclusively with one of the largest and most successful market wizards.

How you trade, what you trade, and the frequency of the trades you make all come down to who you are as a person, not what you know about a specific financial instrument. That's the gaping hole in the training of traders. If you take away anything from this book, make it these points:

1. Trading profitably is about mathematical expectation.
2. Knowing yourself is more important than what you know.

Business school doesn't address either of these. Who you are, not what you know, determines how well you do. It is said that persistence and determination are factors in success. Those are emotional characteristics, not black-and-white facts.

You might be attracted to commodities futures because you've read about Bill Dunn and his systematized approach to trading. But how do you know which trading method is best for you? How do you approach trading when you've heard that "you can't time the market," yet traders are doing it every day?

You may not know a thing about commodities futures, but you can overcome this lack of technical knowledge with effort and the appropriate education. Once you learn the technicalities of commodities and systems design, you have to learn to trade. How is it that Dunn can trade dozens of commodities profitably, but others can't? It's not because he has a magic system. What he does have is a financial system that's congruent with his emotional makeup—that's the key to long-term success in managing risk.

You can argue that at the heart of successful trading is the trend, up, down, or sideways. Trends in stocks and futures occur over all sorts of time frames: intraday, daily, weekly, and monthly. Do you buy, sell, or trade options in sideways markets to profit? These are all technical and intellectual endeavors, and you can learn them. Knowing them only on an intellectual basis does not equate to successful trading. You still need to come in from the dark and get to know yourself.

It can come, as it did for me, through yoga and meditation, and also from spending a few years in a Trading Tribe.[1] For Mike Bellafiore, it's found in running the big loop in Central Park at 5 AM. For others, it's playing the banjo to get into a meditative state. Most of this book came to me from sitting still and keeping a journal over the years with notes from the classes I've taught and insights I've accumulated about myself. I am not afraid of who I am or what I sound like. Best of all, I don't care what others think about me. I am immune to peer pressure. In that regard, I am fearless. I have surrendered to the fact that I am an emotional being and that my emotions run my system. I have cut the throats of all the pink elephants that lived off the fat of my land over the years. I have my feelings as friends and allies, and I speak about them frequently. In speaking with me, people think I have candor. I just think it's emotional integrity.

This emotional knowledge that you need to increase your sense of self-awareness is attainable. You can say that what you need most to trade consistently profitable is already inside your brain. You just need to understand what and why you do the things you do. That might require you to question your entire belief system and where you got those beliefs, which can be scary. Like Leonardo da Vinci, who said something to the effect of "David was always inside the marble—I just set him free," you can do that for yourself. And you don't need anyone's permission. You can give it to yourself.

So, with self-awareness in perspective, you can take a new approach to trading. Instead of saying, "I want to trade cocoa like Michael Marcus," you can say to yourself, "I want to experience the same feelings that Michael Marcus experiences when he is trading at his best." This gives you insight on why an MBA might not give you the edge that you thought it would if you want to pursue trading as a profession.

Most successful traders know where they will exit losing trades before they enter them. They know what the losses feel like, and they embrace them. You can ask yourself which of the results you envision feels best to you emotionally. Pros know the answers to those questions, and that is how you will know what to do. Your job as a trader is to identify the best time frame for the security and merge that with your emotional constitution, energy level, capital commitment, leverage, and your need for liquidity.

Each trader's personality and emotional constitution is as unique as his fingerprints. That's why you'll see one trader who's great at trading options but can't trade commodities futures. It's also why Warren Buffett doesn't trade currencies or commodities very well; it's certainly not because he's not smart enough. Nor is it because one asset class is riskier.

"I want to experience the same feelings that Michael Marcus experiences when he is trading at his best."

I know commodities traders who work with futures contracts more conservatively than investors who buy and sell mutual funds. For example, one trader I know makes trades based on the notional value of the futures contract. To trade one gold contract, he needs $140,000 in the account to cover the full value. That's 100 ounces multiplied by the price of the contract, which, as of March 2011, is about $1,400 per ounce. With the margin for COMEX gold at almost $7,000, it may escape some to think in terms of keeping large fluctuations in their account to a minimum. Trading based on the notional value achieves that, and some traders may find it emotionally appealing. Compare that to the trader who funds his account with $20,000 and trades gold. The swings in the two account balances will be staggeringly different, and each will have corresponding emotional attributes. In my experience, the concept of "intentions equal results" is true from a conscious and subconscious level. Then it follows that the emotional responses to the large up-and-down fluctuations in the account are as much of a goal as the potential to make money.

But this is part of the futures trader's style. It's what feels comfortable to him. For him to trade this way, he has taken leverage out of the equation. How you trade and manage risk comes down to your emotional makeup—that's what draws you to your favorite security, just as you're attracted to a certain kind of person. But when you look at your trading results, it's not the security or how you trade it, per se, that's the attraction: it's the feelings that the combination of each give you. What differentiates one trader from the next over many years isn't the ability to trade commodities or stocks; it's the differences in the emotional trends they are willing to experience. These trends are formulated and developed from your childhood. Often they relate back to what you learned about money from the people closest to you, usually your parents and family.

Table 2-1 gives characteristics of the types of securities that you may be drawn to, such as equities, options, commodity futures, and interbank foreign exchange. Read down the columns, not across the rows.

TABLE 2-1 *Emotional Trading Barometer*

Potential Leverage	Holding Period	Daily Energy Level	Liquidity	Overall Temperament
1:1	Fraction of a second	Low	Low	Brain dead
2:1	Tick per trade			Not present
4:1	Minutes			Low energy
10:1	Days			Calm and placated
20:1	Weeks	High		On edge
200:1	Months	Jolted	High	Lit up like a Christmas tree

We are all pleasure seekers, and so much of what traders do is about pleasure. You might think that they just want to avoid pain. In general, that is true of professional traders, hence their ability to absorb small losses. This is not necessarily a skill that the new trader has upon beginning a trading career, but it's one that has to be learned.

Marry the wrong instrument with your emotional make-up (which, in the short term, is fixed), and you'll have a bad trading experience. For example, if you are normally a low-energy person and you try day trading foreign exchange (forex) with 200:1 leverage, the results could prove disastrous and you will get a lot more out of trading like this than just the whipsaws in your account. As Ed Seykota remarked to me once, "It's the S&P 500, not the Daytona 500."

Here's a detailed example.

You read about a certain trader in the book *Market Wizards,* and you identify with his philosophy. That's intellectual, but it's your entry point to trading. You have no idea what's before you, but somehow you're excited—that's emotional.

You open a margin account with $100,000 to trade commodities futures. This is your money. All futures trading is done in the margin account, as opposed to a "cash" account, which is for stock trades. You have a system that you call "yours," but in reality, it's a store-bought system that you understand intellectually. It's yours on some level. The system includes basic rules on keeping losses small for trading single contracts of gold. Over the first two weeks, small losses offset your gains for the first five trades in a row. Each one makes you more frustrated. You know that gold is going up—at least, that's what everyone is calling for—but you're not making any money. Had you not offset these first trades, they would have become larger losses. You quietly thank God that you're not down 20%.

Curiously, you find it difficult to put on the sixth trade. Your first five trades were losers. Even though the computer spits out what you should do, your emotions are flowing like a live wire off a high-voltage power line. "I thought systems were supposed to annul my emotions," you say to yourself. That's not the case for you.

You are not alone.

Over the following two weeks, you earn it all back with one trade that just takes off for reasons you don't understand. Your account is up 10% net in the first four weeks, and you still don't know what you're doing—but you're doing it anyhow.

The account has performed positively and your rules have worked in the short term. What's going on here? Is this a good system, or are you just lucky? Here are the results:

- There's not enough data to say whether the system is good or you're just lucky. You're probably lucky in the short term.
- You were initially drawn to trading for the excitement.
- You're glad that you took small losses because they could have been much worse. You feel relief to this day.
- You were correct only once in six trades, less than 20% of the time. Not exactly accurate, and you're ashamed.
- You feel relief that you got out of the losers quickly, but you're frustrated.
- You made money, but you don't know why. You're puzzled.
- You found religion by thanking God—this may be religion or ritual.

- If you closed your account and took the money, you have more than you started with. This made you grateful and happy.
- You're scared because, when you took all your losses, you felt strongly about never making any money. You also felt scared taking your next signal because you lacked confidence, both in yourself and in your system.

In the paradigm of "Intentions equal results," the emotions you derived from your trading were as much the result as the gains were. So relief, frustration, puzzlement, excitement, and shame were also goals. And this was for an account that was up 10%.

The emotional model also has a chronology, in order:

- Excitement
- Relief
- Shame
- Further relief
- Frustration
- Puzzlement
- Ritualistic familiarity
- Gratitude/happiness

This is your emotional system running in the background of all that you do. Like a computer operating system, if you had a Control+Alt+Delete, it would allow for all that would come up on your Task Manager. You, too, have a lot running in the background.

If you don't like the model, you have to change your behavior or change the rules. Meditation can be a big help in quieting your mind. That's where the fun begins. Unless you try to better understand what the rules of your system mean to you emotionally, you're going to derive similar feelings each instance you run your system. If you join a Trading Tribe, you get your emotional trading systems to converge. Otherwise, you will never be exempt from strong feelings when trading. You can think of your trading rules as "emotion generators," with entry, exit, and position sizing as catalysts driving the system.

Each indicator that you add to your trading system tries to preclude you from your feelings about loss and uncertainty.

Taking it a step further, each technical indicator that you add or remove from your trading system has an emotional payoff; the net profit and loss is incidental. As you develop your trading career, you will have to work on your emotional system while also developing your trading model. Because your emotional system is always on, it's impossible to separate the two. It's running whether or not you are aware of the emotions and feelings.

Each indicator that you add to your trading system tries to preclude you from your feelings about loss and uncertainty. If nothing else, you may find yourself using the technical indicators as little emotional bandages to cover up your true feelings about uncertainty. Professional traders live with the uncertainty because, in the end, they can never remove it entirely. All you can do is take consistent small losses and make sure that no single trade defines your career.

Nothing can teach you about your emotional constitution like putting real capital at risk. Then you're managing risk and attempting to keep your losses small. Imagine the emotional shock that the buy-and-hold crowd is in for when (a) the stock market crashes or (b) their assets fall into a protracted drawdown, probably right when they need the money most. How reckless it is for the buy-and-hold investor who has no idea what's in store by not keeping losses small. Who can predict where things will be in the expected buy-and-hold time frame when assets are supposed to grow—perhaps by retirement or for college education or to take care of parents?

Part of your growth involves surrendering to the fact that you have zero control over what happens or the results from all your hard work. You have zero control over the variance between your hypothetical results and what actually happens when you begin trading and managing risk. This is much more challenging that it might appear. You can say, "I know that I do not know," but the emotional intelligence and self-awareness to live that expression is very different from knowing it intellectually. It makes sense logically. But when you're faced with testing all the intellectual information you've filled your brain with, you cannot escape the emotional learning curve that trading brings. Surrender, therefore, becomes one of your strongest characteristics and personality traits.

I trace my emotional learning curve in Chapter 3, "My Tuition." My ability and my willingness to surrender has been the greatest "indicator" of my own growth. I do not become emotionally invested in the outcome of any trade (or any life event, for that matter). Things go wrong, and we can't control many of them. If Barton Biggs and Al Harrison can be at times so incorrect in their fundamental analysis, and if Bernard Madoff and Philip Bennett (Refco) can dupe the best auditors and private equity firms of our time, how do you think you can outfox the overall market that is omnipotent and omniscient?

Only when you can merge your emotions with your trading rules and combine the trading results with your feelings will you have developed your inner voice, the only "person" you can count on consistently. You then will have aligned your emotional system with your trading system.

The key is to know where and when you are getting out before you put the trade on. This is crucial for survival. If you have to make a decision under duress and figure it out while you're hemorrhaging cash, you will eventually bleed out. In the words of Jonah Lehrer, "When you overthink at the wrong moment, you cut yourself off from the wisdom of your emotions, which are better at assessing actual preferences. You lose the ability to know what you really want."[2]

Because of the need to be correct, you might let a trade become an investment. Reluctance and regret have killed more traders than black swans.

People trade for more than the profit motive. When your feelings are the goal (the desired outcome of trading), all you can do is study yourself and determine your motive. This is where yoga, meditation, or participation in a Trading Tribe becomes invaluable. You will always follow the trend of your feelings first; the gains and losses are the symptom—the runny nose of the cold, so to speak. They are incidental.

Successful traders time the market to exit losers quickly. This flies in the face of everything you've heard on TV about how timing the market doesn't work. This is confusing, which, in turn, makes you more frustrated. Who do you believe? With a mentor or coach, you can begin to trust your feelings and see things for what they are. You can make your own decisions about what you specifically can and cannot accomplish.

If surrender is beyond you right now, consider that ego and hope will keep a trader in a losing trade for what could be a long time. Because of the need to be correct, you might let a trade become an investment. Reluctance and regret have killed more traders than black swans. *Coaching tip:* If you don't take the small loss today, you risk total loss of your capital or career tomorrow. Surrendering does not mean that you give up or quit. Nor does it mean you've lost the battle. It does mean that you are willing to emotionally accept small losses in the short term because you surrender to the fact that it is impossible for you to know all the possibilities of why a position goes against you. How do you know you're wrong? Easy. You're losing money on the position. Surrendering requires that you hold out an olive branch to your emotions while you trade. They want to help you—all you have to do is let them.

The most successful traders surrender their egos to not knowing the frequency or magnitude of any trend. They quiet their mind and follow their inner voice. They throw out their degrees and any sense of self-importance. They are passionate about the markets, and they remember one thing: *Gains look like gains only to the extent that you keep your losses small.* Most of the world can't do it, so on some level, professional managers who've been around for decades play the best defense. That's why you don't see them on CNBC with the latest stock picks: It's not about stock picks.

Surrendering is knowing that things can happen in the markets for reasons that you don't understand. Surrendering is knowing that you're still powerful because you can come back and trade tomorrow. Surrendering means stopping and listening to your feelings and emotions and embracing them because they teach you something about yourself. The wisdom found in your inner voice cannot come from a book, TV show, or trading course. You can get to it safely from taking a yoga class, meditation, or quiet exercise.

Winners never quit, but quitters have more equity because they stop trading when they become entrenched in a losing streak.

You may be emotionally tied up in the old adage of "Winners never quit and quitters never win." Every trader I've ever studied with or been mentored by has taken time off from trading to regroup. Think of it as a sabbatical. Winners never quit, but quitters have more equity because they stop trading when they become entrenched in a losing streak.

All feelings are good when they teach you about yourself.

When you know what motivates you emotionally, you are your own best mentor. At the same time, this provides judgment without slotting your feelings as good or bad. All feelings are good when they teach you about yourself. When you listen to what they teach you, your emotions are your allies, not your enemies. *Surrender* should become your new favorite word.

Chapter 3

My Tuition

I paid a great deal of tuition to develop my inner voice, mostly in the form of trading losses. You learn the most from your losses. Winning trades do nothing for you in this regard except boost your ego.

If you are ever asked, "How would describe your level of intelligence?" you might answer, "Above average." This is probably emotionally gratifying to say, despite not having a single, measurable heuristic as proof. I'd probably say the same thing, although nowadays I have what's called "Social Proof"—recommendations on LinkedIn, letters from deans, and positive reviews from students. I'm smart enough to know that I can still vaporize cash very quickly, and I own the fact that I am not immune from becoming a bonehead. As a trader, my profit and loss statement is the best reflection of my inner voice.

When I began my career, I made several errors in my own trading that certainly didn't look "above average." In fact, the mistakes I made were the same rookie mistakes that I teach everyone else to avoid. Looking back, most of them were downright hilarious, although they didn't seem so at the time.

You can avoid two easy errors:

- Don't over-trade.
- Don't overleverage your account.

If you can avoid these two errors, you will go a long way toward avoiding total ruin. Out of the game. Done. No equity. No margin. No career. And lots of excuses.

When I first began trading, there were no exchange traded notes (ETNs), exchange traded funds (ETFs), or

Internet stocks. I had blue chips, tech stocks, and commodity futures. Most of these also traded options. Then, like now, Intel (INTC) and Microsoft (MSFT) had great influence on the NASDAQ Composite Index. Yet they were nowhere near becoming Dow components, as they are today. Naturally, with few great names in tech to trade, many of us focused on the theme of the day, known as W-Intel, the marriage of Microsoft's operating system Windows and Intel's newest chips.

Earnings season was up, and INTC was about to announce its earnings per share number. I had a hunch that if that number was positive, the stock would see a sizable move because the trading range (the near-term high and low prices) had been tight for the past few weeks. Traders had a few ways to play the potential upside for INTC, which at the time was trading around $70 per share. I used an options position because I didn't want to tie up a large portion of my equity in a long position in the stock. I could benefit on the upside by spending $4,000 of my equity on options, whereas the same position in the stock would tie up $70,000. I read all the research from my firm and every other firm on the street, thinking that was going to give me an edge. No other Internet source at the time was available for traders to get the line on earnings, nor were there online communities for sharing advice—no StockTwits, for example. I had to rely on my research and the evil, false, and manipulative whispered number.

I read all the research from my firm and every other firm on the street, thinking that was going to give me an edge.

A whispered number is an alleged inside line on the earnings of a firm, perpetuated like a stock tip. It's usually baseless and provides the earnings whisperer an air of having inside information, or some type of knowledge that the firm is deliberately guiding everyone on the street to a lower range, but with the full knowledge that the actual number released will be a material number of cents per share better than the projections of all Wall Street analysts. But I was ignorant and didn't know exactly how to refute the young chest-pounders who perpetuated the whispers, using it as a form of currency for political capital in their clique or to impress others, or profiting in a "pump and dump" scheme. I felt like I was part of the crowd knowing the whispered number, but it didn't help keep losses small.

I had another hunch that INTC might split its stock. It was trading at the same price level where the firm had decided to split its shares in the past. Firms split stock for the sole purpose to make it more affordable for investors to buy a round lot (100 shares) of the stock. I had noticed that stocks tended to jump in value after stock splits were announced.

I owned the 70 calls (call options that give the owner the right to buy INTC at $70 per share) in my portfolio at a cost basis of $1.50 per contract about 10 days before the earnings announcement date. Lucky for me, the stock began trading higher over that time. On the day before the earnings announcement, my calls were just over $3 per contract. I was up 100% on this trade based on the premium paid, and I hadn't even gotten to the announcement yet.

When earnings day came, the market closed and I sat in utter stillness to await the news. I had interpreted the paper gains of 100% as a foreshadowing of more profits to follow. Based on that, I'd inferred that I'd make many times my money. Keep in mind, there was no aftermarket, save for what was known as InstiNet (Institutional Network)—no Electronic Communication Networks (ECNs) or anything. The number reported was significantly higher than the street guidance. While my colleagues hit the phones looking for a quote from one of their buddies on a desk, I had an "in" with an analyst I'd caddied for and was listening to the earnings conference call. The analysts on the conference call mentioned that the stock was trading up $7 on InstiNet in the aftermarket and that the firm, Intel, had, in fact, announced a two-for-one stock split.

I had all night to fantasize about how the stock would rage at the open the next day: a better-than-expected earnings number, stock up significantly on InstiNet, and a split. What a dream!

I had all night to fantasize about how the stock would rage at the open the next day: a better-than-expected earnings number, stock up significantly on InstiNet, and a split. What a dream! "Who knows how high this thing can go?" I remember telling all my friends and clients on the phone that night. I was up, on paper, almost ten times my original investment while the rest of the world was liquidating its shares overnight on the InstiNet system. I got to the office much earlier than usual the next day. I needed to celebrate my big win and enjoy how the morning would unfold. I wanted to experience it all—smell the smells and watch all the folks roll in and wonder how their days would go. I had a built-in good day: I had a built-in profit and limited emotional downside, given all the positives for Intel that the Western world was going to wake up to.

In those days, you couldn't see the price changes nor activity from the overnight trading session. All you could see was the previous day's close. The effect of the split, higher-than-expected earnings, and forward-looking statements focused the retail investors who hadn't owned the stock the day before into buying up shares that morning. As you may have guessed, I didn't have a clear exit plan for my trade. Professional traders did. They sold on InstiNet after the earnings announcement, and they sold into all the retail investors' buying power that morning.

At that moment, I began to hear Linda Blair's voice in my head during that scene in *The Exorcist*—the one with the crucifix in her bed—and it occurred to me that something was rotten in the state of Denmark. The ticker tape was acting funny. It seemed stuck at +$7. I was just about to calculate how much I'd make if it went up another $10 per share. I still didn't have the price to sell my calls at which I'd be both emotionally and financially happy—and then waves of selling hit the tape and took away all the overnight gains. I was so stunned, I couldn't breathe. So I did what all rookie traders do when they can't breathe in that situation: I went downstairs to smoke a cigarette.

I learned that the professional traders (guys who have a wise inner voice and are smarter than those of us who are smarter than average) had been accumulating stock and watching the same charts that I had been watching—but they had done so for a much longer time. As the stock opened in the green, they had a strategy to sell into that strength and take extra profits. They planned on buying it back cheaper after all the profit-taking. I had no such exit strategy—just daydreams of my inner excellence. Up to that point, I had only a coasting strategy based upon hubris. By not defining a clear exit strategy, I had inadvertently become an investor with an options position.

By not defining a clear exit strategy, I had inadvertently become an investor with an options position.

I got out, still making 100% on the trade, but it was the proverbial "set of steak knives" while the pros that got out at the top drove off in the first-prize Cadillacs while thanking their inner voices. The conversation I had with myself was much different: "This will never happen to me again. I will always be ready to act if the market gives me such a rare gift like this again. I can think about how to get back in once I've taken profits and I'm back safely in cash. I'm such a jackass." And I was.

This, as you can imagine, was a 180-degree about-face from not even a full day earlier. I had been up almost ten times my money, yet in the end, I walked away with only a double. I see this trade as a failure because I choked on the exit. I mishandled my taking of a profit. My emotional sense of self suffered a catastrophic hit as I watched my equity bleed away. I knew what to do technically, but my ego and emotional immaturity as a trader had me all twisted up in the game. I walked home through Central Park, sat on a bench in Poet's Walk, and had what Peter Borish later explained to me was a proverbial "park bench day." The worst part was that because I had to open my big mouth and build up everyone else's expectations about the trade, I now had to call them and tell them that we had done no better than we had been before the news had been released. They were happy with the double, but I was humiliated.

One of the most expensive errors I've ever made, but also one of the funniest, occurred in the early 1990s. An extreme heat wave was just sitting on top of the Great Plains, home of the majority of states growing wheat deliverable against the Chicago Board of Trade (CBOT) contract. Wheat as a crop is a total wimp, but soybeans can take more extreme conditions. Too much moisture for too long, and you end up with a rust fungus. Too much heat, and the arid conditions or drought kills off the crop.

Two weeks before the July 4th weekend, the heat was brutal. I was long on wheat in modest amounts in all my commodity accounts and was making all the money I could dream of as the fear of damaged crops drifted and crept along the floor of the CBOT. As we came in to the last trading day before the holiday weekend, I was sure the contract was going to sell off. Most of the traders on the floor would take their gains and go home with no open positions. Everyone in the market was long on wheat, and all they needed was one sprinkle or break in the heat over the holiday weekend, and the contract would have traded down its allowable limit (the maximum it can trade in one day). The contract had moved about 80¢ ($4,000 per contract) over that two-week period of time, and I had already taken decent gains out of the long trade. Now I was going to test my knowledge of how the floor acts. Obviously, I thought I could take on the traders in Chicago looking at one another on the floor from my desk in Manhattan.

I decided that going short would be the play as a deluge of selling would surely hit the tape in the last 30 minutes of trading; we'd be good for at least 5¢ to 10¢ of downward pressure. My reasoning was that anyone who was long would have already been long. No one would be initiating new long positions before a holiday weekend; there was too much uncertainty. If one floor trader started selling, I figured they'd all pile on and sell.

My risk on the short sale was 2¢ above my short entry, and I was figuring on as much as 5¢ to 10¢ of profit if the contract sold off like I thought it would. So I called my floor trader and sold 50,000 bushels of the July contract with about 30 minutes left in the trading day. But nothing happened, and the selling didn't show up.

The wheat market, like all commodity markets, is a living and breathing mechanism. The sum total of all commodity trading in wheat will give you its pulse and vital signs, not just for one month, but for all the expiration months. I was about to learn this. What I didn't notice was that the floor was selling a deferred month's contract short—in this case, the December contract—to establish a hedge against the long July contracts. That's why the July contracts were not depreciating. The floor traders were selling heavily, but not the contract I thought they would sell, and it was all happening under my nose. In the end, they had created a spread position by being simultaneously long the July and short the December contracts. (In a short sale, you can make money when the instrument declines in price. In this scenario, the professional traders had two contracts in their portfolios of the same commodity over the weekend: They kept their July contracts long but sold the December contract short, in the event that something negative happened. The losses would be offset by the short December contracts. With this strategy, traders wouldn't get hammered for large losses by being long only the July contracts.)

I was so emotionally invested in making a quick 10¢ that I had neglected to look at what was happening in the entire wheat market, not just the front month. (The front month, also known as the near month, is the first contract for expiration that you can trade in the current calendar. Contrasts with deferred month, or deferred contracts, may be many months away from the front month.)

I was so emotionally invested in making a quick 10¢ that I had neglected to look at what was happening in the entire wheat market, not just the front month.

With six minutes left in the trading day, my strategy did not play out. We weren't losing anything, but the beer at the South Street Seaport had sharper selling than wheat did in Chicago that afternoon. I called the client and said, "Nothing's doing. Let's get out and come back next week." The client said, "You're right. Let's just sell it." Time was of the essence, as we had five minutes to the close of the market. With my wheat trader on the phone in my other ear, I said, "Sell 50 July Market." "Sold," he screamed back into my ear. Then came a moment that can only be expressed as the cartoon scene when Wile E. Coyote is trying to blow up the Roadrunner, and he's got the live grenade in one hand, but he's got the pin stuck on his finger of his other hand. He says, "Stunning! Isn't it?" Realizing that the grenade was about to go off—which it eventually did—I saw that I had not "covered" or offset my 50,000 bushels with a buy order. I had actually doubled-down and was now short 100,000 July wheat contracts with about five minutes until closing.

We weren't allowed to call the floor in a panic and undo error trades, which would have been the smartest and least painful thing to do. No, we had to go to the operations desk and get someone with Commissar Authoritarian Wisdom to electronically journal the trade to the firm's error account and then offset it there, all while the market was still moving, but nearing the close. This gave me great motivation to run as fast as possible to the operations desk.

In a moment of hilarity, I ran like heck from my desk and turned the corner, blowing past the men's room and the front door to the office, a blind spot where a gentleman was walking through the front door. I took him out with an open-field tackle reminiscent of the late Oakland Raiders defensive back Jack "The Assassin" Tatum, and kept going. I had no time to stop to see his strewn papers still floating in the air like that bird feather at the beginning of the movie *Forrest Gump*.

I got to the operations desk, and the person who had to help me was smoking and talking on the phone, with her back to the window. I pounded on the bulletproof glass to get someone's attention, and she slid the window open and said, true as God, "My daughter just broke up with her boyfriend. I'll be with you in a minute, Bubbs." Bubbs! I went from being a self-described great grains trader to an actor cast in a David Lynch movie. My life had been reduced to a scene from *Twin Peaks* in less than five minutes.

I went from being a self-described great grains trader to an actor cast in a David Lynch movie. My life had been reduced to a scene from *Twin Peaks* in less than five minutes.

We did all the journaling, and in the end, it cost me about $1,200. Some of it was to pay for the error on the trade: We had to make the client whole and give him the buy price at the time of the error trade to cover his short position, and I had to offset the loss to the firm in the error account.

This $1,200 error was my tuition for an important lesson. If I was going ahead with the late short sale, I should have written down the order, repeated it to the client, checked it against the existing position on the books, and finally called it in to my trader. I had become cocky because I'd had a great two weeks of trading. Being cocky is an emotional problem, not a technical one. In the overall scheme of things, I should have gone to cash at the open and taken half a day. I could have read a good book on the train to Spring Lake. But this story gets funnier. I happened to be "broker of the day," that random fool designated by the branch who gets called by everyone wanting free stock quotes and copies of prospectuses of hot stocks that they can't get shares of. The guy I tackled at the front door would become my client. He was a walk-in and didn't have anyone at the firm already handling his account. We became good friends, and he eventually opened 16 accounts with me and we made a lot of money together, mostly with listed and OTC stocks—but no wheat futures.

Of course, no story about cutting your teeth would be complete without a story about relying on your firm's fundamental (or "funny-mental") analysis. Mine was at the hands of analyst Jonathan Cohen, who was so talented that our firm referred to him as the Special Situations analyst. The year before I first heard of him, his research picks were up about 105%, the way Wall Street firms do their accounting.

A few dozen Stanford Ph.D.s would go to the Amazon Rain Forest and shake down the natives for their witch doctor/medicine man methods.

I'd met Cohen at my branch a few times, and he came across as a highly intelligent and very well-spoken guy. I liked him. Besides, this anecdotal story is about how I mishandled risk and its effect on my inner voice. Cohen didn't do anything except what he was supposed to do: analyze companies and provide research. One of the stocks he recommended had what he referred to as an "ethno-botanical approach" to drug discovery. A few dozen Stanford Ph.D.s would go to the Amazon Rain Forest and shake down the natives for their witch doctor/medicine man methods. Their firm, Shaman Pharmaceuticals, would partner with them in the process of discovering new drugs. After all, "aspirin was discovered this way," I remember either him or Shaman's then-president Lisa Conte telling us. It seemed like a great approach, and one that was socially responsible. Like "fair-trade" coffee, the concept of "sharing" in the drug discovery process made me feel good. But this feeling and trading have no business dealing with one another.

One of Shaman's drugs was a salve for genital herpes. The drug in Level II studies showed efficacy in allaying the symptoms of herpes sores. Unfortunately, as an investment, the folks who studied the Phase III clinical trials didn't think so, and the stock tanked on the news; my position's value was cut in half. All was not lost, however, because the firm had two promising drugs for unrelated illnesses: Provir and Virend. But neither panned out, so the stock suffered despite Cohen's bullishness. My cost basis was between $6 and $7 per share, and now the stock was now about $3 and change. I can remember having dry heaves all night, but I hadn't a drink in me. I was pacing the floor like an expectant father. I thought, "My clients trust me with their money. How can this happen? They can lose 50% without me. What value am I bringing to the table? How will they trust me after this? I am a complete failure."

The first rule of handling someone's money is that if there is bad news, they have to hear it from you.

That night, my nerves were shot and I was in complete disbelief that I could lose 50% of an equity position's value in the matter of moments. I had cut my teeth trading commodities, after all; no one said that this could happen with stocks. The next morning was horrible. The first rule of handling someone's money is that if there is bad news, they have to hear it from you. If you call only to let them hear you pound your chest, they will have no respect for you. I had to call them before they heard it from Jim Cramer or Dan Dorfman.

The only upside to the story is that the initial position was no more than 5% of my overall equity, so I was being hard on myself, to some degree: It wasn't like I was nailed for a 40% hit to 100% of the equity. Yet I think that when someone entrusts you with their money, you have to treat it like a newborn child. Even if they can afford to lose all of it, you still need to preserve it—if for no other reason than to keep your own sanity.

Thomas Edison said he failed his way to success. I seemed to be doing that, too, but it didn't feel very good when I strung my feelings together.

Thomas Edison said he failed his way to success. I seemed to be doing that, too, but it didn't feel very good when I strung my feelings together. Yet I had set it up just as I had wanted it. I had no one to blame for my failures or to share in my successes. I had to own up to the whole lot of it. I had no room for ego or blame here. If you don't have a sense of humility, you're dead before you start. Your level of technical proficiency is a distant third in this race.

One more thing about Shaman: This was the last time I ever made a trade that had any element of approval or legislative risk. When the risk is binary—yes or no—your best bet is to use options; that's the only way you can define your risk and limit your losses. It was my last time for penny stocks also. Stocks are that cheap for only one reason: No one wants them. And if you argue about stock splits, you're missing the point. Public companies do not enact a 20–1 split in good times or when they think things are looking up. Its' more like, "Look out below." Although the legal definition of a penny stock is a price of $5 or lower per share, I think that stocks trading under $20 are penny stocks, too. I think of stock prices between $5 and $20 as those best traded through Long Term Equity AnticiPation Security (LEAPS) options.

The price always tells you the truth.

Incredibly, that feeling of a firm being socially responsible had me way off-center. I have never again made an investment based on these feelings. I trade to make money, not to be judge and jury for a firm's strategic plan. Don't let a firm's ethos take you away from solid research and risk management. The price always tells you the truth. Leave the social responsibility to the board of directors or the CEO. Your job is to manage risk. Don't bring political activism or political correctness into your portfolio. There's not way for you to quantify that as a risk.

One major takeaway from this is the importance of position sizing. "Thank God," I can remember saying after the Shaman incident. My saving grace was that I hadn't loaded up on the stock. I remember how much I liked that feeling, despite making several mistakes. This good feeling of appropriate position sizing showed up again many years later, this time in a commodities trade. In late 2003, I was trading live cattle when the news of mad cow disease hit the tape. "Mad cow disease" is the slang expression for bovine spongiform encephalopathy (BSE), a fatal neurodegenerative disease in cattle. Like most trend followers, I was long live cattle at the time. Figure 3-1 shows a chart of February 2004 live cattle contract I was trading at the time.

FIGURE 3-1 *The effect of mad cow disease on cattle prices.*

Chart from FutureSource.com.

Those dots running down the middle of the page don't indicate that my printer needs to be cleaned or the toner levels checked. They signify limit moves, the daily maximum price that a contract can move before the exchange halts trading. You cannot offset your position; you're stuck in it. Because I was long, good risk management dictated liquidating my position. But the contract was locked down at its daily limit, so I couldn't get out. No lower boundary limited how many of these days could occur in a row before the selling stopped. You have to know this before you trade commodities. I survived this bout of mad cow disease because my initial position was set at such a level that I could withstand several consecutive limit moves against me. By trading smaller, you forsake lower upside, but you have the benefit of smaller downside when something unpredictable like this happens. I had prepared for mad cow disease emotionally by learning from my Shaman trade. This was my inner voice at its best.

Chapter 4

Two Traders' Paths

For the new trader, the book *Market Wizards* delineates some of the most remarkable success stories in almost heroic terms. Each trader interview includes technical examples to learn from. I've forgotten how many times I've read the book and how many times I've reverted to its sections—surely hundreds of times.

The traders depicted in *Market Wizards* and Schwager's follow-up book, *New Market Wizards,* are often regarded as statistical survivors. Many of them might not have been around to become *Market Wizards* had they not developed their own inner voice by learning from their technical and emotional mistakes. The difference between investors who are unlucky and unknown and these market wizards lies in how they traders recovered from their mistakes. Statisticians tell you that if you line up 1,000 traders, you can pick the top 14 and write a book about them. But you have to reassess the role of luck and randomness when you evaluate their successes in developing their inner voices. If developing their inner voices was the deciding factor (and intentions equal results), the market wizards manifested their own destinies. This is not random.

If you rewrote the preface of *Market Wizards* from an emotional standpoint, the book would have a much different vibe, but it would still be a rewarding read. You could read a few pertinent emotional lessons, such as these:

- A trader borrowed money from his mother on several occasions and had to take tranquilizers to offset the agony of missing a trade.
- A maverick cotton trader lost 90% of his capital on one trade by playing macho man with the market.

- A media-shy music lover lost 50% early in his career by getting too cute with the market.
- An engineer pioneered computerized trading rules but couldn't stick to them.

Each trader went through an emotional hazing. Each paid a great deal of tuition in the form of losses. No one got a free pass. If you pursue trading professionally, you won't, either. That's how you develop your inner voice.

Most of the wizard tales derive from one of several emotional experiences that traders endure, bringing them perilously close to a zero or negative account balance—the point of no return. Almost all the wizards subjected themselves to wild swings in their equity and a minimum of a 50% drawdown; that figure seemed to be the minimum requirement for entry. (A drawdown is a decrease in your trading account, your combined realized and unrealized losses. For example, if you traded your account from $50,000 to $108,000 and then it decreased to $70,000, you would have a $38,000 drawdown.)

Michael Marcus is widely regarded as the greatest commodity trader at Commodities Corporation—and probably in the world—during the 1970s and early 1980s, Marcus regularly garnered over 100% return rates and sometimes upwards of 1,000% during his tenure at Commodities Corporation. He made the transition to trading after working as a fundamental analyst at CBWL Hayden Stone. Yet Marcus might not have been anointed Pope of Trading had he not survived several emotional "coming of age" trades. As he put it, "The markets were so fertile for trading then that I could make plenty of mistakes and still do well."[1] But markets go through hot flashes, and then fertility ends. That's when the mistakes begin to hurt not just financially, but emotionally—and one mistake, in particular, hurt Marcus very much.

Commodities captured the inflationary pressures prevalent in the 1970s, as he explained:

> Everything was going up. Although I did very well, I did make one terrible mistake. During the great soybean bull market, the one that went from $3.25 to nearly $12, I impulsively took my profits and got out of everything. I was trying to be fancy instead of staying with the trend. Ed Seykota never would get out of anything unless the trend changed. So Ed was in, while I was out, and I watched in agony as soybeans went limit-up for twelve consecutive days. I was really competitive, and every day I would come into the office knowing he was in and I was out. I dreaded going to work, because I knew soybeans would be bid limit[2] again and I couldn't get in.[3]

In an interview for this book, Marcus revealed some painful and traumatic experiences from his upbringing. He had been forced to fend for himself emotionally from a very young age. His father was stricken with cancer when Marcus was 10. Although his father sought treatment physically, he refused to address it emotionally with his son. He continued treatment for five years before he died, but he lived at home. He didn't say goodbye, and he maintained that, in his own mind, he didn't have cancer. He spent his time in self-absorbed denial. He went to work but didn't have any energy left for the family by the time he got home at night and on the weekends. "We went from doing everything on weekends—touch football, baseball—to nothing...no contact." Marcus was 15 when his father died. His mother also checked out emotionally, so he didn't have either parent to rely on for emotional support. Marcus took solace in being a phenomenal student. That was a feeling he loved, given how sad his family life had become.

Marcus was a Merit Scholar in high school and did well enough to become accepted into John Hopkins University. "I was a phenomenal student, unbelievable," he says. Marcus believes, though, that he didn't manifest all his gifts until he got to college.

Like his protégé and former colleague, Bruce Kovner, Marcus had real intellect and took great pride in being the smartest student around. He liked to read for days on end at the library. "I really lived inside the library," he says. "I might as well have put it down as my post office box. I belonged to a fraternity, but I was not really fraternal until Saturday. Otherwise, I was in the library or class."

"I really lived inside the library," he says. "I might as well have put it down as my post office box. I belonged to a fraternity, but I was not really fraternal until Saturday. Otherwise, I was in the library or class."

Feeding his brain was his sole focus because of its emotional appeal. "I was thrilled to learn and study these great books," he says. "I felt it was a privilege to read, and it felt great to me." Eventually, Marcus took so many extra classes at Johns Hopkins that he almost completed a triple major. "I was a liberal arts major, but I was one course short of an English major, one course short of a philosophy major, and one or two courses short of a psychology major. I concentrated on those three subjects."

Not surprisingly, Marcus regularly debated his professors in the middle of a lecture, disrupting the entire class in the process at Clark University in Worchester, Massachusetts, where he thought he'd get his Ph.D. in psychology, but not before completing active duty in the National Guard.

Marcus began trading in 1970 just after graduating from John Hopkins, having been inspired by a newsletter called the *Chester Keltner Letter.* As with his studies, Marcus dove into trading and studied it diligently. After losing his $1,000 Bar Mitzvah money, Marcus cashed in a life insurance policy and traded that $3,000 up tenfold to $30,000 just as he arrived at Clark to attend his first semester of studies. He explained:

Not surprisingly, Marcus regularly debated his professors in the middle of a lecture, disrupting the entire class in the process.

> I found myself much more interested in my positions than in trying to develop my doctoral thesis. I found this alarming and concerning because I loved my studies at Johns Hopkins and ... lived for them. [B]ut here ... in graduate school, I was no longer interested in them. I knew what

> it was like to be passionate about my studies, and I no longer was. All I could think about were my positions and going to my broker's office in Worchester to see how they were doing.

It's not a stretch to understand a top student's nature to want to take on the market intellectually. Marcus was used to being right all the time—and being more right than anyone else in his class. Each year, he was one of the top two students in his class, and he was inducted into Phi Beta Kappa. Trading was his next intellectual proving ground to conquer, but not before he went through some painful experiences.

Marcus left Worchester for New York City in January 1971. "I lost everything—and I probably owed my mother, my brother, and [my] girlfriend money," he says. "I was broke and I needed a job. I was walking along on Park Avenue and I saw a billboard that said, 'Job Finding Seminar Inside.'" As it turns out, author Austin Marshall was giving a seminar on "How to Get a Better Job," which explained the process from the hiring manager's perspective. It struck Marcus as an unlikely but extremely beneficial lesson. "I saw wider implications in this lesson for trading the markets. It didn't matter if my fundamental take was true anymore. The charts had to reflect my ethos, and the market had to behave in a favorable way, too," he says. This analogy sheds some light on the saying, "The market can stay irrational longer than you can stay solvent." By marrying technical analysis with his fundamental take, and looking for further validation from the market, Marcus was on the way to making history.

I would be pulling my hair out and looking for a window to jump out of. Ed would say, "Well, markets go up. Markets go down. Today they're down."

The final skill Marcus needed to develop was his emotional reaction to the markets, and this came from reading the tape and getting a feel of crowd reaction to news. This was not a skill that came naturally to Marcus, despite his great interest in psychology.

In recounting his inability to keep his emotions in check, he contrasted his behavior against that of his colleague and mentor Ed Seykota:

> Ed had the ability to contain his feelings when a position went against him, [whereas] I couldn't do that—it was always a difficulty for me. I would be pulling my hair out and looking for a window to jump out of. Ed would say, "Well, markets go up. Markets go down. Today they're down." He used to smoke a pipe in those days, even as a young guy, and I used to see puffs of smoke coming out of his pipe. I'd notice sugar was locked limit down, and I'd ask him, "Say Eddy, are you still in that thing?" And he'd puff on his pipe and say, "Yep." He would always be so contained and tough, and I learned from that. I was never as contained as Eddy, but he helped me in that direction. He'd be getting destroyed on a position. I'd be living in the bathroom somewhere. But I traded more like Amos Hostetter by incorporating fundamentals and technical

> analysis and watching what the crowd was doing. Eventually, I learned to have a great feel for the markets, and that had a lot to do with settling my expectations in my trading.

Before developing his phenomenal feel for the market, Marcus had to pay an emotional tuition as well as financial one. He took profits too early on a soybean trade and watched in agony as it continued to rally. This type of rally especially hurts when you need the money (see Figure 4-1).

Source: CME Group

FIGURE 4-1 *The move in July CBOT Soybeans 1977 went from $7.50 to $10.50 per bushel in about seven weeks. The $3.00 move represented a 40% increase in prices, yet with the implied leverage and the size that Marcus traded, it would have added several hundred percentage points to his portfolio over the same time. The sell-off from June to expiration would have been as profitable also. July 1977 Expiration CBOT Soybean contract (1 contract = 5,000 bushels).*

Eventually, I learned to have a great feel for the markets, and that had a lot to do with settling my expectations in my trading.

Marcus didn't just dread a missed opportunity. He found the experience much more aggravating. A trade of this magnitude can make your year, return-wise, if not your career. In what he described as the low point in his trading career, Marcus eventually took a sedative to dull the mental anguish of missing the large move up in soybeans.

Marcus had originally taken a mild sedative to calm his anxiety, but it didn't work. He then turned to Thorazine:

> I was getting on the subway to go to work. The subway doors started to close as I was getting on, and I started to fall down ... I wandered back home and just fell through the doorway—it was that strong. It knocked me out, and I missed work that day. During those two weeks, I was constantly on the verge of being wiped out. It was the worst two weeks in my whole life. I went to the office each day just about ready to give up. And this wasn't from losing money! It was from not being in a very potentially profitable trade.

TIP On another trade, Marcus loaded up on corn and wheat by posting $50,000 on margin–his $30,000 plus $20,000 that he borrowed from his mother. He lost $42,000 on the trade.

> **TIP** Marcus lost $2.5 million in about five minutes on a currency trade. He got out to avoid having to watch the $2.5 million loss grow. Then he "had to endure the disturbing experience of watching the market recover its entire fall."

You can follow his wisdom. Explore your feelings about needing to be correct and examine how you feel about being wrong. To me, this is more important to know than "how to trade soybeans like Michael Marcus." As Marcus says, "In the end, losing begets losing. When you start losing, it touches off negative elements in your psychology; it leads to pessimism. Trading requires an intense personal involvement. You have to do your own homework, and that is what I advise people to do." Your homework is to learn from Marcus's emotional lessons. In the process, you will develop your inner voice of trading.

Marcus learned a great deal from these emotional experiences. His approach was to meditate and undergo several forms of therapy. While we shared stories about our upbringings and events that had traumatized us, he says, "That which you make conscious, you can begin to heal. By sharing it with others, you make it conscious. You can't get more conscious than by telling someone."

> "That which you make conscious, you can begin to heal. By sharing it with others, you make it conscious. You can't get more conscious than by telling someone."

His history motivated him to learn more about himself, the fundamentals, the technicals, and how the market acts, the three inputs that he incorporates in his trading today. Chief among them was to rigorously manage risk. Despite having some emotional rides as volatile as the markets he was trading, Marcus was persistent and was determined to become the world's greatest commodity trader—and he did just that.

Marcus became the Pope of Trading by harnessing his emotional pain and spiritual evolution. Although he traded profitably early on in his career, by the time he began to feel free of his childhood pain, he had already spent approximately two-thirds of his life "empty," as he says. Not until Marcus found meditation and dove in headfirst did he began to feel that he had a connection to the universe and could free himself from his pain.

On the other end of the trading spectrum is Bill Dunn, of Dunn Capital. Whereas Marcus to this day employs fundamental and technical analysis along with a feel of the market, Dunn is purely systematic. He computerizes his entry and exit rules, as well as his position sizes. If anyone can be called the Patron Saint of emotional discipline, it is without question Dunn. It's one thing to upload an algorithm into a computer, but it's another to follow the trading signals to a T without having the emotional need to override the trading orders. Marcus's trading style is said to be discretionary, whereas Dunn's is systematic. One isn't better than the other; each trader has to discover the best individualized approach. Marcus embraces his feelings and incorporates them into his trading style. Dunn relies on his mathematical model to derive his orders, despite his strong feelings. Unlike Marcus, Dunn has no publicly known emotional breakdowns to describe that shaped his career. He has never blown up, nor did he have a defining experience in the markets that ultimately shaped his career the way Marcus did with the soybean trade.

Discipline is just acting in accordance with your goals or your agreements with other people, despite the strong impulse you may have to act otherwise. It all comes down to integrity, whether you use a computer to run your model or not.

Like Marcus, Dunn is one of the most academically intelligent traders I know. His approach is that of a scientist. Dunn has a Ph.D. in theoretical physics from Northwestern, and he worked as a university professor at one time. Despite having the brains, Dunn uses neither discretion nor gut feel in his trading. I first met Dunn when I interviewed him for an article that I wrote about him, called "Unbreakable," for *Trader Monthly* magazine. A few years later, he and I filmed a longer two-part video interview for my blog, Martin-Kronicle.com. Dunn is the chairman of the board of the Reason Foundation, the entity that publishes *Reason Magazine,* so he and I had another thing in common, the magazine's motto: "Free minds and free markets."

"We are 100% systematic...there fore, zero discretion," he says. "That is a very difficult thing to live with when you just get started because there is [sic] all sorts of information coming into you from the market and your psyche."

Despite being fantastically intelligent and well read, Dunn has a discipline that I have not witnessed in any other trader. "We are 100% systematic ... therefore, zero discretion," he says. "That is a very difficult thing to live with when you just get started because there is [*sic*] all sorts of information coming into you from the market and your psyche." Whereas Marcus emotionally needs to derive a thesis and prove it right in the market, Dunn uploads the data into his computer each day and relies on his mathematical model to decide when to enter and exit the markets he trades. "Systematic" means that Dunn has studied decades of data and has found an equation that calculates when to buy and sell commodity contracts. Only when certain conditions are met does he make a transaction. Dunn uses the term *discretion* to mean inputs other than his computerized model. Marcus uses the term *discretion* to describe his modus operandi. You can say that the very thing Dunn tries to avoid, Marcus takes solace in. One way works for Dunn, and another way works for Marcus. Both methodologies are successful.

> "'Bill, you trade the system and *nothing else*,'" he recalled. "That generated juices in my emotional system, and I was talking to myself ... 'I know I'm too late. I know I'm hanging on too long. Look at this loser here—I should liquidate this position.'"[4]

If Dunn didn't have the necessary discipline, his clients sure made it clear to him what he was to focus on with their money. "When I was starting out, I was told by clients, 'Bill, you trade the system and *nothing else,'*" he recalled. "That generated juices in my emotional system, and I was talking to myself ... 'I know I'm too late. I know I'm hanging on too long. Look at this loser here—I should liquidate this position.'"[4]

Even when Dunn hears his inner voice speaking to him, he reverts to his trading rules as he's done for the last 34 years and relies on the scientist in himself. "Our system was the distillation of all the past data that I could analyze, and that system was the best thing I knew to do for today and tomorrow," he says. "The temptation to make discretionary trades was not very strong because I knew I shouldn't. I'm enough of a scientist that I overcame my emotions and I told myself to let the market activity play out."

One thing Dunn is not doing is reading and trading off the scrolling, albeit distracting, breaking news at the bottom of the TV screen. "The best I can do each day is follow my rules," he says. "So if it didn't work out today, big deal. There was no guarantee that it would work anyway. We never override the system."

Dunn's model does not allow for discretionary trades and that has been the case since 1974. "What's the point?" Dunn insists:

> Why do people think they are smarter than the market long term? What gives them that confidence? I guess people feel dumb if they can't predict what the market is going to do in the short term. They're too proud to admit they don't know what to do when they're wrong. They don't have the capacity to understand the digits that are scrolling by on the bottom of the

television. I don't. It's too much noise. That's why we rely on our system.[5]

Another interesting aspect of Dunn is his outlook on dealing with potential clients. "We interview them as much as they seek information about us," he says. "There's no ambiguity—we tell clients that they have to be with us for the long haul, or we do not want their money."

> "Typically, the trader does not want to have to deal with the client's feelings."

This is an important turning of the tables. "Typically, the trader does not want to have to deal with the client's feelings."[6] By putting his clients through an interview process, he limits the emotional upheavals that can occur between a client and a manager. Most of the time, the client holds a lot of political power because, early in a trader's career, the client is the one with the money. If you don't have any bullets, you can't shoot your gun. By putting potential clients through this process, Dunn has less probability of dealing with client drama. Market volatility can evoke strong emotions from clients, and they can lever those feelings into your trading model if you're not careful. You need to draw boundaries with them.

Dunn's process on vetting clients shows a giant rate of return by minimizing the drama between manager and client. The good news: He has 34 years of consistency behind him and no sign of blowing that record.

Your emotional life will evolve, and your trading needs to adapt to different market environments. However, market environments don't change like the seasons; you don't get a "heads up" on the environment changing. Nor do you for your emotional life. It just evolves. You can be much more in tune with it if you meditate or take yoga. That is what your homework will be for the next 20 years: Measure the convergence or divergence between your trading system and emotional system, because both will change.

> Market volatility can evoke strong emotions from clients, and they can lever those feelings into your trading model if you're not careful. You need to draw boundaries with them.

Whatever you believe about Marcus or Dunn, it's certain that they have not only the courage to persist through sheer determination, but also the courage to look inward and determine that they needed to execute emotionally to become great traders. One thing I know is that each one is an A+ student in self-awareness—and that school is always in session.

When you approach investments, trades, and relationships from an emotional risk/reward standpoint first, your life becomes much easier. You minimize your emotional losses. When Mike Covel interviewed me for his book *Trend Following,* I told him, "If my clients don't get what I'm doing, then I may need new clients, or they may need T-Bills. Their money-drama is not part of my system."[7] The market wizards have set a standard, but not because they made gigantic trading gains or worked at famous firms. They had to wrestle with themselves and negotiate with their inner voices of trading. Make your feelings your friends and allies or, as Yoda said, "Suffer your father's fate you will."[8]

Chapter 5

Conventional Wisdom/Market Timing

Conventional wisdom is emotional comfort food.

A book for traders and risk managers about emotional wisdom and self-awareness needs a benchmark to compare the various levels of risk against. In this chapter, I take a look at what buy-and-hold investors must be going through emotionally.

To me, owning something without having a defined exit point is reckless behavior. I believe this is true for any type of trader or mutual fund investor. People work too hard for their money, and there seems to be a big disconnect between the potential for substantial loss and risk management on Wall Street.

Owning something without having a defined exit point is reckless behavior.

Contrary to what you may have read, stocks are not the best place for your money over the long haul, neither emotionally nor financially.

The wisdom of mutual fund trader and market timer Gil Blake is often overlooked for some of the more famous traders depicted in Market Wizards. He said that "trading is probably more of an art than most people want to believe."[1] This must seem out of left field if you were raised with slogans such as "You can't time the market" and "You have to buy and hold." Blake wasn't a trader in the strictest sense. He was a mutual fund market timer, and up to the time of his interview in the *Market Wizards* book, he had not had a losing month.

Price and volume are expressed in bundles on a daily, weekly, and monthly basis. You can also study *intraday* data, the daily data broken down into subdivisions of the hour. These time bundles can be 1, 3, 6, 10, 15, 20, and 30 minutes. Professional software customizes the data so that price and volume are expressed in the desired time frame.

Picking the right time frame has a lot to do with your personality and, on a deeper level, your understanding of trust. If you don't trust that your stop orders will get filled, you have no other reason to watch the screen all day when you use daily time frames. Brokers have incentives to execute your trades exactly the way you want them executed: It's called a commission.

Blake said the novice trader needs to complete several steps to become a successful trader. These begin with finding the trading vehicles, strategies, and time horizons that suit your personality. Blake didn't say to find the ones that were "most profitable." He didn't say to find the ones that had "the highest mathematical expectation for a trade." And he didn't say to find the ones that were "the easiest to market to investors or that had the best Sharpe ratio." He said to find the ones "that suit your personality."

Investors who hide their feelings behind that "buy and hold" nonsense of "I'm investing for the long term" are parroting what they've heard someone else say. They're denying their fear. Fear-based models have never done well on Wall Street. These investors have no idea what the long term is, nor do they have any clue about what the long term will bring. Buying and holding is the greatest gamble you can take with your money.

An investor feels good today by saying, "I'm doing this for the long term," but the feelings that come as a result of those actions today may be discomforting.

Investors who hide their feelings behind that "buy and hold" nonsense of "I'm investing for the long term" are parroting what they've heard someone else say. They're denying their fear.

Humans are very poor at estimating and give themselves too much credit.

Let's take a look at why I feel this way (and think this way, too). When I first landed on Wall Street, the saying was, "The S&P 500 has historically returned 12.25%, dividends included." Clients who took this advice might have indexed their money away. From 1990 to February 2011, the S&P 500 returned 8.91% total return (6.65% without dividends), far below what was suggested and modeled for. In fact, the S&P 500 returned not even three-quarters of what was projected—72.73%, to be precise. Despite the fact that a 30-year-old client at the time is now 51, that client hasn't hit his goals, despite being much closer to retirement age and probably having most of his biggest income-earning years behind him. For all such investors' "head in the sand," "I'm in this for the long haul" racket of buy and holding, they need to take on more risk to reach their goals, assuming that their goals haven't changed. Let's see where the opportunity cost of buy-and-hold ran amok.

Research on the companies included in the Russell 3000 conducted by Blackstar Funds (now known as Longboard Asset Management) found that most stocks lose money over their lifetime. You've been told that stocks are the best long-term place to grow your money. Not so. Take a look at Figure 5-1.

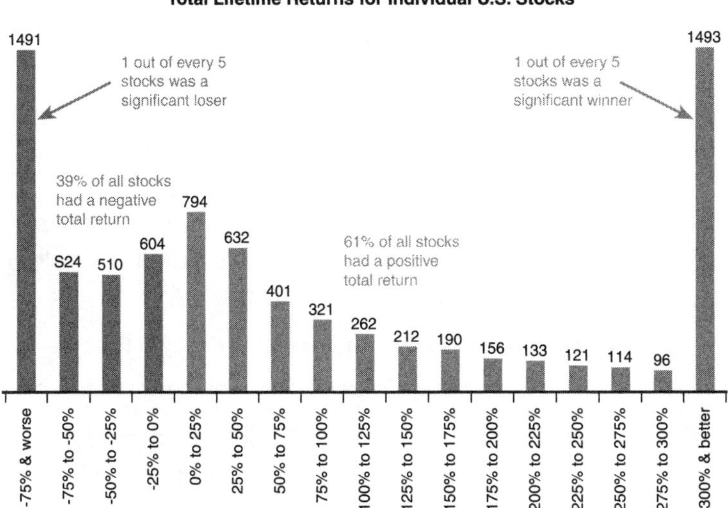

Source: Cole Wilcox and Eric Crittenden, Longboard Asset Management

FIGURE 5-1 *Stocks' lifetime total return.*

The breakdown on stock returns on 8,035 stocks from 1983 to 2007 is as follows:

- Thirty-nine percent of stocks had a negative lifetime total return. That means two out of five go bust.
- Eighteen and a half percent of stocks lost at least 75% of their value. That means one out of five is horrible.
- Sixty-four percent of stocks underperformed the Russell 3000 during their lifetime.
- One out of five is one of the stocks that's touted and spoken about in the mainstream media.
- The median compounded annual return was 5.1%

How does that make you feel? What do you think you should focus on if this is the case?

When I see advertising and marketing from the mutual fund management companies, and compare it to how the majority of stocks actually perform, it gives me the sense that the mutual fund industry is more of a lobby or political action committee than an investment firm. Take a look at the compounded returns for stocks in the following chart (see Figure 5-2).

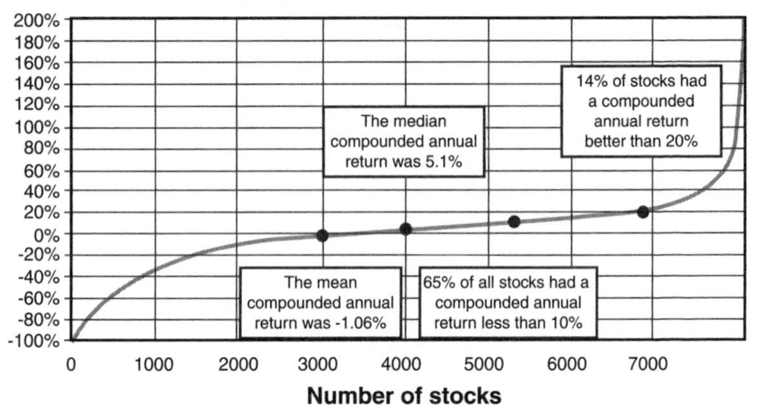

Source: Cole Wilcox and Eric Crittenden, Longboard Asset Management

FIGURE 5-2 *Compounded annual returns for individual stocks.*

And when you sort all stocks in the study from least profitable to most profitable, 75% (or 6,000 stocks) had a total return of 0%. And these are the stocks in the index.

If your answer to my hypothetical question is "I need to focus on stock picking," you are mistaken.

When the majority of stocks lose money, you need to focus on "not losing." That means keeping your losses small by using market timing to exit unprofitable trades at a predetermined level. A good example of this is Bill O'Neil's CANSLIM methodology. He gets out of losers at 8% from the purchase price. The following chart, Figure 5-3, graphically depicts just how drastic it is to be a buy and holder or a stock picker and not focus on keeping losses small.

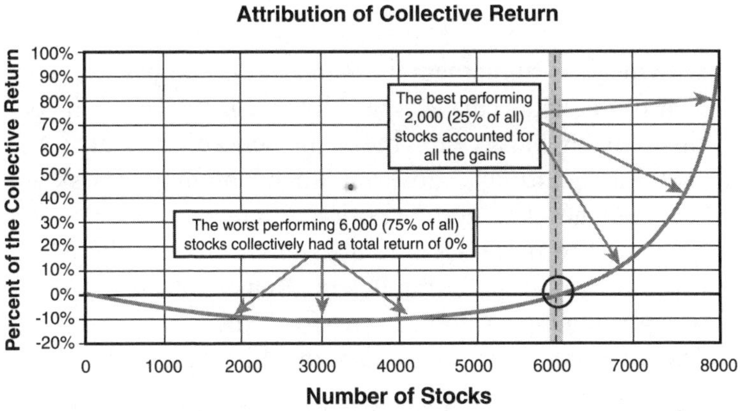

Source: Cole Wilcox and Eric Crittenden, Longboard Asset Management

FIGURE 5-3 *Attribution of collective return.*

I'm curious whether your mutual fund manager has any definable edge, given these definitive results. My guess is, he or she doesn't have any edge, but instead has a great wholesale representative who can convince your financial advisor to recommend certain funds. Fundamental analysis won't help, either.

When the majority of stocks lose money, you need to focus on "not losing."

> When you hear managers say, "We sell when the fundamentals change," do not give them a cent to manage.

Don't trust "averages"—they make otherwise bad things seem reasonable. Don't be reasonable with your losses. You probably won't see "average" when you look at your portfolio. Your eye is trained to look for the biggest winners and the biggest losers. The latter had to have been small losers before they grew up to the big losers they are today.

When you hear managers say, "We sell when the fundamentals change," do not give them a cent to manage. This is especially true if they have lined their "team bios" with big-name schools and professional designations. Those don't help you manage risk if the manager has zero emotional intelligence or self-awareness, or if he operates in an environment where he can't act emotionally intelligent. Remember, seven out of eight managers don't outperform their benchmarks. This is true despite their educational backgrounds.

Tudor Investments founder who was also featured in Schwager's Market Wizards, Paul Tudor Jones said, "Prices move first and the fundamentals follow. Al Harrison, who was vice chairman of Alliance Capital, was buying Enron all the way down "because the fundamentals were there." And he was the vice chairman of the firm at the time. You won't have his resources. The market, not devotees of Graham and Dodd, will tell you what your stocks are worth.

The once-hyped and touted Munder NetNet Fund did so deplorably that Munder merged the Fund with another, and it's now known as Munder Growth

Opportunities. This does a few things. First, it gets rid of the data and the hideous price chart. Take a look at the chart in Figure 5-4.

FIGURE 5-4 *Despite massive marketing during the internet boom, Munder's Net Net fund was a "net net loss" for most investors.*

Second, Munder Management doesn't have to keep reported deplorable returns and the massive hit to capital (drawdown) from trading losses and from client attrition. However, even the new fund has about 15% of the assets that the NetNet fund had in its heyday.

When you and your advisor don't have the resources traders have at their disposal, what makes you think that stocks are the best bet for you in the manner you're investing in them? In other words, if 6,000 stocks make

0% over their lifetimes, "buy and hold" and "long-only" are clearly not the way to go over the long term for stocks. You need something more substantial and much more reliable: technical analysis or a trading model that will limit your losses so that your winners can grow exponentially.

Although I'm a bigger fan of *Market Wizards* (the first book) by a long shot, Jack Schwager's second book, *The New Market Wizards*, has a worthwhile chapter that you probably missed, because it didn't have a name attached to it. It was called "Zen and the Art of Trading." On the fold opposite the three-page chapter was the following text by Jack Schwager:

> Time and time again, those whom I interviewed for this book and its predecessor stressed the absolutely critical role of psychological elements in trading success. When asked to explain what was important to success, the market wizards never talked about indicators or techniques, but rather about such things as discipline, emotional control, patience, and mental attitude toward losing. The message is clear: the key to winning in the markets is internal, not external.

These words are the most insightful of either of the books, yet they've not shown up in the lexicon or of the "favorite quote" sections in the blogosphere. I've never heard a fundamental-based mutual fund manager utter these words. The goal is to "gather assets" rather than "manage assets."

Why? Look at the math. If you have $1 million and you lose 10%, you're off $100,000 and your account balance is $900,000. The manager still earns 0.50% as a management fee. If the manager lets you lose 10%, the management fee falls from only $5,000 to $4,500. Big whoop. Therefore, managers aren't incentivized to keep your losses small, because it's not critical to their revenue stream.

> The message is clear: the key to winning in the markets is internal, not external.

If you don't have a sense of who you are, it won't matter whose lessons you learn or whose training you purchase. Like the supergenius who can't write or speak well, this advisor might as well be mute. If you're filling your head with all this great material but you don't calibrate it and conjugate it with your emotional system, you will find yourself taking an emotional path divergent from your trading ethos. Even the buy-and-holder needs to learn to time the market, if for no other reason than to keep losses small.

In this regard, investors can take away some emotional and technical wisdom from traders. Successful traders learn or are born with the ability to be comfortable in very uncomfortable situations—as in managing risk. Their clients can't do it, so that's why they hire the traders. Investors don't like the feelings of having to make lots of transactions without some level of certainty that it's okay to do so. They also need emotional validation that it's okay to take small losses to protect their capital. Taking small losses keeps traders around for decades. Investors can take this to heart.

Yoga positions are challenging and, in some cases, uncomfortable. With the help of an instructor, you may find yourself in a challenging pose (called an asana) and hear your instructor tell you to relax in it. "Just breathe and be there." This is great training for traders who must endure a great deal of uncertainty all day, all night, and potentially all weekend.

> Investors don't like the feelings of having to make lots of transactions without some level of certainty that it's okay to do so. They also need emotional validation that it's okay to take small losses to protect their capital.

To get a sense of who you are and to develop your self-awareness, one approach is to begin meditation or a yoga practice. Yes, it sounds like a granola flower child speaking, but that's how I did it, and I don't know any other way. You can join a Trading Tribe, but that's a hit-or-miss proposition, depending on the Tribe you join. I was lucky to have Ed Seykota sitting directly to my left. You also need a mentor to help you develop your trading model and style so that it fits with your emotional constitution. You can read all the "how to" books you want, but until you address this, you're destined to repeat your bad trading habits.

Every trader I interviewed for this book told me that they had some form of spiritual practice, even the day traders. Mike Bellafiore likes to go for an early morning run. And I mean *very* early morning. It's not uncommon for him to run in Central Park between 4 and 6 a.m. I asked him, "Mike, why so early?" He said, "Because I gotta get it in, and if I don't make it a priority, it's never going to happen." On a side note, he chooses not to run with headphones on. Many of you might equate heading to the gym, the treadmill, or wherever with your MP3s blasting. Not for Mike. "I can't possibly gain any clarity if I have to actively listen to someone singing."

Bellafiore's business partner, Steve Spencer, has his own approach to gaining inner wisdom. It's much different that Bellafiore's, but just like a trading system, it works for him. "I have been doing yoga for almost eight years now," he says. "I started with my sister, but now I do it mostly on my own around New York City."

My guess is, you're not going to see anyone on *Fast Money* talking about yoga or "sitting in quiet conference with the infinite," but you ought to. I have no doubt that everyone on that show does something to zone out and get their minds off the market and trading, even if it's to go out and have a smoke. Maybe it's not something the viewers of their great show are interested in for the short time they have together each night, but my guess is that if I got one of them on a podcast, we'd find out very quickly.

I was introspective to begin with, but once I hit the yoga mat, I lost myself in the process, which is exactly what you're supposed to do. I took classes with five or six different teachers. I eventually studied with Erich Schiffmann and Jorgen Christiansenn once I had the insight to understand what they were talking about and to gain the wisdom to deepen my practice. It didn't make much sense to visit with Ed Seykota if I hadn't had to sleep with one foot on the floor at some time because I was afraid of a position I had on.

I know yoga and meditation isn't for everyone, but my thinking is, if you give it a try and it doesn't affect your trading, at least you experienced yoga. Plus, this book would lack integrity if I downplayed the role yoga and meditation have had on my life.

Admittedly, I didn't really get yoga until my fourth month of practice. I dove in head first and went to class obsessively four to six times per week. It helped that I lived only three blocks from the school, so, armed with an "unlimited" membership, I was hell bent.

I read *Autobiography of a Yogi,* by Paramahansa Yogananda, after about six years of yoga, and I enjoyed it so much that I bought the audio book read by Ben Kingsley. I had gone to the Self Realization Fellowship for their midnight meditations on New Year's Eve, and I ran into a good friend at the Lake Shrine. We immediately began a meditation group, which we've continued for the last six years.

I never was a gym rat. I know many traders who like to hit the gym or go for a run, but I don't care for either. First, gyms are meat markets. Second, I don't like running—it's too high impact for me. But if you get in the zone from hitting the gym, by jogging around the reservoir, or riding your bike around the small loop in Central Park, stick with it. Whatever you do, think about how consistent you are in your efforts. Your non-trading system is a leading indicator of how you'll run your trading rules, whether they are discretionary or purely systematized, or a combination of both.

When we say that trading is mostly psychological and emotional, your sense of self-awareness is the only tool that you have. That's why traders fail—they lack this skill. They don't know what makes them tick. Then they try to marry themselves with a trading system, and it's a moot point. If it happens, it's entirely by luck.

> When we say that trading is mostly psychological and emotional, your sense of self-awareness is the only tool that you have.

Your sense of self-awareness is as unique as your fingerprints. I can't change your fingerprints, but I can tell you that yoga and meditation have affected mine. And they've been around for 5,000 years. That's the best I can do.

"But Mike, I want to make $1 million right now," you might be saying. "I can't wait for another three years." Well, look at it this way. Malcolm Gladwell wrote in his book *Outliers* that it takes about 10,000 hours to become an expert at something. Even if you make it into SMB's training program and they grubstake you to trade live on your 26th day, you're still an amateur in my mind's eye.

Yes, I'm also aware that you want to show everyone how smart you are by making prescient calls in the markets, but you can do that with a blog and Twitter, if you want. Don't lose anyone's money trying to be Joe Market Timer. Also be aware that opinions are the currency of analysts. I presume that if you're reading this, you want to be a trader. All you have to do is subvert your ego and keep your losses small.

You're just getting started, and all you're doing now is learning what it *feels* like to manage real risk. Why not enjoy the process of becoming a professional trader? What's the rush? The markets will always be there. You can trade international markets, too. What do you think you're going to feel when you make $1 million dollars?

Using Gladwell's math as a guideline, if you worked ten hours a day (quality hours, not labor union hours) five days per week for 50 weeks, you'd reach the expert level in eight years. You have a long way to go. Be present and enjoy the journey. You learn the most by being present. I know that when I'm present, I accelerate the my learning process because I'm focused and I have the most clarity I'm going to have in that moment.

When people want to jump the gun and accelerate their careers too fast, they blow up because they haven't achieved the emotional knowledge that goes with managing risk. If you can't tolerate the pain of waiting or growing at a steady pace, you can use those feelings as an entry point into your Tribe meeting.

When people want to jump the gun and accelerate their careers too fast, they blow up because they haven't achieved the emotional knowledge that goes with managing risk.

People allocate money to you to trade because they don't have the mental toughness to do it themselves.[2] Think about it. Are you going to tell me that someone who has a college degree cannot understand the basic tenets of defining a trend or recognizing the positive slope of a trendline? They hire you to pull the trigger the way you do because you don't freak out in managing risk—or do you?

Everyone in this business has what I call a "park bench day," when they go sit in Central Park and ask, "Why the hell am I in this business?" You may feel terrible. You have a losing position on. You either get out of the business or get out of the trade. Most people can't get off the bench and get back into the game. The great traders have had many park bench days, but they manage to get off the bench and get back into the game.

That's the life you choose in your paradigm of personal responsibility. I got where I am because of circumstances, not because of my degrees. Borish continued, "I'd rather dig one hole 10 feet deep than dig ten holes 1 foot deep. A little knowledge is the downside of trading—the cost of implementing that knowledge—you think you know something and lose money much faster than you ever could."[3]

The trading aspect is a noncommon human feeling. We look for support or a pat on the back. We need to get A's going through school. There we have ingrained in us the need to be "right." Trading is contradictory to academic life. Alpha is not about being right—it's about making money. Most people want to be right. But there is no limit to how high you can go in life if you don't care who gets the credit.[4]

Studies have shown that momentum is far more important than asset allocation as a factor in returns. How are you using that information in your investment thesis? How is your financial advisor making sure you are in the best sectors or vehicles to capture the momentum? Asset allocation captures beta. Anyone can get you that.

Do you like the feeling of telling everyone how great you are at something? Or how proud you are of yourself because of this position you have on? Do you find yourself walking around the office telling everyone that you have a big position in a security that had a move in your favor? In my experience, those feelings are great indicators that it's time to take your profits. The other side of that emotional coin is the humility that you'll need when you have to explain how it all went wrong. That's if you have the guts and integrity to be honest with them. Neither of these feeling will auger well for you in your trading career. If you need attention, take acting classes and get on TV, but don't trade. You'll likely attract all the wrong attention if you do.

Entry prices are for your ego. You want to be buying when others are buying and shorting when they are, too. It's one thing to make money; it's another to keep it. It's yet a third—and better thing—to make money and keep it with little or no drawdown. Risk-adjusted returns are the key selling feature. No one is going to ask you whether you own Google (GOOG) to the extent that you can't manage risk with real money on the line. That guy who talks about his basis in GOOG and how he nailed this and that trade is the real big cheese on Wall Street. He'll never have the humility to tell you what he learned from his losses. He wants you to think that he's never had them. He's the worst type of Wall Streeter. He'll be out of the business within two years. And you'll inherit his accounts with portfolios of garbage stocks with large unrealized losses. The sad part is, his clients are bigger dopes than he is, and they'll go with him because he's a nice guy.

Your job is to keep your losses small. Focus on that, and don't let some salesman psych you out. He's getting all his best ideas from other guys who are cut from the same cloth he is.

Potential client: Why should I give you money?

You: I will lose you less. (value proposition)

People are drawn to the vehicles that will give them the emotional return they seek, whether they're aware of it or not. So when you're building out your trading system or set of rules, make sure that your real needs are getting met, or you may find yourself with results that reflect your true emotional goals.

An unintended consequence does not have to have the frequency of a 1-in-100-million probability. It has to happen only once. What happens to you when a 1-in-100-million chance event occurs in the first 250 trades of your career?

People are drawn to the vehicles that will give them the emotional return they seek, whether they're aware of it or not.

Chapter 6

Emotional Blind Spots

No algorithm can quantify emotional intelligence or self-awareness.

Unfortunately for those of us who are in the business, some of the most famous people associated with trading are the ones who have garnered the most press for horrendous and sometimes criminal activity. Names such as Kerviel, Madoff, Hunter, and Leeson conjure up images of some of the most fantastic losses of capital that the world has ever seen. You'll never see a headline that says, "Trader Made 12% for 30 Years with Only 2% Drawdown: Clients Kiss His Feet, Rename Their Children, and Hand over Their Wives Willingly." But you've seen how many pair of shoes Madoff owned.

The top brass of some quantitative trading firms—the Quants, as they're called in the excellent book of the same name by Scott Patterson—were affected by large, unexpected losses. Boaz Weinstein, Cliff Asness, Peter Muller, and Ken Griffin incurred large financial hits to their equity during this time. That's the black and white of it. I believe this was due to emotional blind spots in their trading models; they believed their math was omnipotent and could explain all the market's behavior. However, they were being myopic. Because of how their models were programmed, they assumed that things would stay the same. Things didn't, and it was the Quants' responsibility to know that. For a group of guys who love Texas Hold 'Em poker, they misplayed their hands terribly. Sometimes you have to fold a strong pair, such as pocket aces. These firms went along as if nothing could beat their pocket aces.

These firms went along as if nothing could beat their pocket aces.

As great and mathematically elegant as their quantitative models were, their firms (Saba, AQR, PDT, and Citadel) took massive losses. With the subprime morass unfolding, brokerage firms were calling on their clients for more margin collateral. Because many of these firms and their funds held similar securities, they were all getting margin calls. It was a house of cards in which you had to take a card from the bottom to put onto another house of cards that was on the verge of collapse itself. Everyone had to grab from the bottom to close at the same time, so speed mattered. If you didn't grab your card quickly enough, it would be worth less moments later—sometimes much less. This is the effect of a margin call. Managers have to liquidate collateral to come up with the funds to satisfy margin requirements. The manager cuts leverage and reduces risk, although he is at the mercy of the brokerage firm. These requirements must be met by the end of the day, at the latest. It becomes a game of chicken among the managers who are all crowded into these positions. Who will sell first? If they wait too long, and wait for the falling security to rebound, they also may be faced with having to sell more securities to meet the margin call if their value falls too deeply. The margin call is a net dollar amount, not a number of shares.

On top of all this, many of these firms, specifically called prime brokerage firms, have their own prop trading—trading their own capital for trading profits. Not only do they know what must be sold to raise the cash, but they can sell it short in front of the large fund to profit from the impending selling. They're not supposed to, but this is like sneaking a proverbial cigarette in the bathroom. Everyone does it.

The firms' quant models could not position the funds to avoid losses or to make money, as they had done previously. Everything was unexpected. The events were unfolding improbably but not unexpectedly. That's where the models began to fail. They could not bet on improbable events.

To complicate matters further, the managers never expected the government to step in and disallow short selling of financial stocks. This eliminated one of the features of their models, which were totally balanced before the new rule. The funds would buy and sell financial stocks or commodities futures. They would also short-sell the same securities. This is a process of selling something at what you believe is a high price today, only to buy it back cheaper tomorrow, so you are buying low and selling high, but reversing the sequence. Short selling is such a prominent technique for these managers that annulling the ability to short financial stocks is the equivalent of telling Picasso that he couldn't use the color blue. John Meriwether and his two Nobel Prize–winning colleagues suffered a similar fate from a similar blind spot a decade earlier at Long Term Capital Management (LTCM). No one at LTCM expected several "once in a lifetime" events to occur within what appeared to be moments, historically speaking. A self-aware trader has "outs"—options trades or flexibility in decision making, for example. They are never held in a choke hold or full nelson.

To be fair to the Quants, securities regulators annulled short-selling financial and bank stocks in an effort to avoid a run on them. Legislative and regulatory risk is impossible to predict. The Quants didn't just short stocks, but they used short selling in conjunction with other trading techniques. This balanced out the risks these firms were taking, or so they thought. After the short selling was banned, the firms had to trade new models. By creating the ban, the government forced new trading algorithms on these firms. This is a great example of how regulators do more harm than good. However, legislative tampering notwithstanding, the Quants should have cut risk when volatility increased. To do this, a trader cuts leverage or position size. They could have eliminated financial and bank stocks from their models altogether. Had their model not had them so overleveraged, they could have easily offset the risk.

However, legislative tampering notwithstanding, the Quants should have cut risk when volatility increased.

As Ed Seykota would say in his Dr. Seuss–style rhetoric, "Their models worked until they didn't work anymore." Losing money is not illegal, and none of the Quants mentioned did anything wrong. They lost lots of money, client trust, reputation, and track record—but that's it.

The chronology of most blow-ups goes something like this:

- The model/algorithm works for months or even years. The results look fantastic.
- A few years into live trading, the model is treated like an important invention.

- An unanticipated market or sector event occurs. It's publicly denounced as a one-off aberration and "it's over with."
- The manager is flat-footed and is not prepared to deal with the issue. It's not over with internally.
- The media and clients want answers. The manager sticks to his model, suggesting that, from vigorous back-testing, things like this would have been picked up. There is no need to deviate from the current path.
- Sensing the financial icebergs lurking, clients redeem shares, leaving the manager to offset their winning positions, the ones with the most liquidity. The manager holds the highly levered losing positions because they are illiquid. They have a garden full of weeds.
- Remaining investors are not rewarded for their loyalty.
- Fund and firm implosion is moments away. It's never the manager's fault for being blind to the outlier event.

My conclusion is that, for an annual management fee of 2% to 20% of the net profits, today's managers are absolutely responsible for outlier events. They must dodge the ones that will hurt and capitalize on the ones they can gain from.

If you study your history on algorithms and highly levered models, this is the norm, not the extreme. It's a question of *when* something will go awry, not *if*.

However, if you plan for the "if" contingencies, you will have cash on hand, small position sizes, and virtually zero leverage, and you can cut a check to the departing clients from your QuickBooks and wish them well—an emotionally pleasing situation for all. No punching monitors or throwing lamps across the room, unless you like the feeling of doing that.

> If you employ leverage to benefit from small price changes, you are smoking at the gas station.

Most readers (as well as me) will not have the brain power of Weinstein, Asness, Muller, or Griffin, nor the talented analysts and traders they employ. But it goes to show you that no one has a lock on emotional intelligence, and everyone can learn a new lesson. A few of the takeaways include these:

Lesson 1: If you can't define your blind spots, you are not working hard enough in risk management. You and I have blind spots. The more of them we perceive, the more we can do to avoid them altogether or include provisions in our models to take them into account.

Lesson 2: Don't hedge speculative positions. Get out of them by offsetting. There is no such thing as a financial Band-Aid.

Lesson 3: If you can't define your risk because something unexpected has occurred, get to cash as fast as possible. You will think with a clearer head if you don't have money on the line.

> **Lesson 4:** You don't need leverage to become a Commodity Trading Advisor (CTA), hedge fund manager, or professional speculator. If you employ leverage to benefit from small price changes, you are smoking at the gas station. This is my single largest concern for the markets with respect to high-frequency trading (HFT). Overleverage is at the heart of all meltdowns and the collapse of empires.

The Rogues

"The Rogues" on this list have lost enormous amounts of capital for their firms. In each instance, they cost many people their jobs and betrayed the trust of their employers and clients. These men did not act in a fiduciary capacity and did not put their clients' interests first.

- Jerome Kerviel, Societe Generale (SocGen): $7 billion
- Nick Leeson, Barings Bank: $1.4 billion
- Brian Hunter, Amaranth Advisors: $6.6 billion

They put their own egos first, their own aggrandizement. They went for the "hero trade" and, in return, caused catastrophic losses. Two of these firms, Amaranth and Barings, now cease to exist.

When their bonuses were in jeopardy due to their first large losses, these gamblers didn't just double down—they went for broke. They tried to earn back their losses and then some, for the sole purpose of earning giant bonuses or to regain status and emotional victories. This is on top of the fact that they didn't know how to trade; they blew up. Trading is about being self-aware to obtain profits in excess of losses. Gambling is about the emotional payoff.

Not on the list is Bernard Madoff, who, despite having committed a white-collar hate crime and stealing $50 billion, never traded—he just stole his clients' money. He was a sociopath, not a trader.

Making money can be the result of either luck or talent. Since the Rogues blew up, I'm now convinced that they had more luck going for them than talent. Intention equals results. Behavior predicts where you end up.

Intention equals results. Behavior predicts where you end up.

Jerome Kerviel is the most sinister of the Rogues. He falsified so many channels to get his trades through that it was like he was three people at the same time. That takes a special mindset, a virtual chess game in his head. Unfortunately for the bank, the money is gone.

Brian Hunter has to be the most egomaniacal of the group. Hunter decided to allocate between 50% and 65% of his firm's assets in one trade. Rookie stockbrokers know better. I think that Amaranth's principal, Nicholas Maounis should be held accountable, too. To not have firm control over his traders or his clearing arrangement is beyond dereliction of duty. The most basic prime brokerage statement delineates all the positions. How he could raise money after this type of oversight is beyond me.

My take is that Maounis didn't want to take on Hunter emotionally and tell him to cut back on the risk. Maybe Hunter would threaten to leave, leading to bad press. I don't believe that the cause for the losses had to do with the lack of risk control at Amaranth. Amaranth knew where the risk was. This was something being played out between Maounis and Hunter. It explains a lot of why Hunter was given control of his own trading—no one at the firm had the integrity to cut Hunter off.

Maounis was avoiding something emotionally by not taking action and cutting Hunter's exposure. My inner voice tells me that you cannot let any one trader set the tone for the firm, no matter how well that person trades or what strategic advantage you think the trader brings to the firm.

The fact that John Arnold of Centaurus was said to be on the other side of the Hunter/Amaranth trade is not surprising, but it's no consolation. When a trader lacks emotional intelligence and has no inner voice to listen to, he is more of a philanthropist than a trader. He's giving money away, so it doesn't matter who is on the other side of the trade, whether it's one of the world's best natural gas traders (Arnold) or a nobody. It doesn't make a difference. The only cornerstone you get is for taking down the firm, not building it up.

When a trader lacks emotional intelligence and has no inner voice to listen to, he is more of a philanthropist than a trader.

The Federal Energy Regulatory Commission (FERC) has a $30 million suit against Hunter, and the U.S.

Commodity Futures Trading Commission (CFTC) has already banished him and determined that he tried to manipulate the natural gas market. These types of trades cast a poor light on the rest of the marketplace.

Nick Leeson learned his lesson first among this threesome. He proved mathematically that Martingale systems, as they're known, don't work. In those systems, you double your risk level with each loss, figuring that, sooner or later, you'll hit and get back to even. Most often, they are employed while trading against the trend of the trade and end with disastrous results.

Consider an example: Say that you lose $500 on a trade. The next trade, you risk $1,000. If that doesn't work out, you bet $2,000. If that doesn't work out, now that you're down $3,500, you bet $4,000. Like I said, Martingale systems don't work: It's an emotional system of risk management that spirals out of control. Each trade brings financial havoc, which further perpetuates duress. If you trade against the trend with a Martingale ethos as Leeson, Kerviel, and Hunter did, you'll bankrupt yourself, if not the first time you try it, then the second time, for sure. Only random luck is at play when such a strategy works out.

One point to emphasize is that these clowns didn't deliberately trade a Martingale system, but this is what their emotions led them to do, whether they knew it or not. That's how vicious a cycle it is if you don't learn to take small losses and flush your ego. Traders don't think it can happen to them, and then all of a sudden they're emotionally invested in the outcome of a trade. A trader must detach emotionally from the outcome of any particular trade.

Invest in your process and stay out of the results. It's a very sober way to trade and one that will keep you trading—and liquid—for a very long time. The concept of "Win it right back" is a death spiral. Keep your losses small, and you'll never be in one.

What the Dog Heard

Let's see if I have this right: You'd rather avoid the feeling of looking stupid by deliberately locking in a guaranteed small loss today, for the more likely chance of feeling despondent when you lose a larger portion of your capital.

That leads to inaction on your part, and you sit in disgust watching the market take away more of your equity, like a bully. Then you talk about how the market is fixed or rigged, when all the while you had the power to get out of a losing position, but you chose not to. You chose not to do the right thing because you were afraid to feel certain feelings. For the record, you do have the right to not participate, but that's for when you're unsure of what position to initiate, not when it comes to protecting your equity. When you smell smoke, assume that it's a five-alarm fire.

Emotional Math

Avoiding the feeling of looking like a jerk > The feeling of losing all your capital

Unless you plan to make an emotional barometer and establish which feelings you want to feel in specific order, you are not going to be able to take the actions that the professional traders take to ensure that their emotions are in line with their objectives.

Big losers had to have been small losers first.

Trading is all emotional. You are in control. You get to decide when you want to take losses. Losses are both emotional and financial, but your emotions will bring you to action or not. In some instances, you get "knocked" out of a trade and it comes back and goes higher. Here's what that equation *must* look like for you:

> Feeling of safety > Feeling frustrated by taking a small loss and watching the security recover

Why? You can always get back in at a higher price. Don't buy more of a losing position, and don't dollar-cost-average your mutual funds.

Ace Greenberg used to look at Bear Stearns' accounts and just sell the losers indiscriminately. Over the years, when he took over certain trading accounts, he issued a blanket order to "sell anything that's down that we've had for 90 days." Each of the traders interviewed in *Market Wizards* decreed and repeated the mantra, "Keep your losses small."

To quote Jim Rogers, "There is no such thing as a paper loss." Big losers had to have been small losers first. You have to be down 2% before you get down 5% before you get down 10% and so on. Cut your losers at the knees before they cut your throat.

Cut your losers at the knees before they cut your throat.

Chapter 7

You Are the Black Box

"Victorious warriors first win, then go to war, while defeated warriors first go to war, then seek to win."
—Sun Tzu, Art of War

Both professional managers and individual traders commonly use computers to manage trades. They scour the data each day and decipher what to do during the next trading session. These instructions come from very rigorous back-testing, a process by which professional managers and sophisticated individual traders test their rules using historical data. The rules are price based and have been tested using as many as 20 to 30 years of data.

These instructions include how to handle existing positions, what to buy or sell, at what price to take a loss, and, most important, how much of each contract to trade (position sizing).

These rules are like a macro on a spreadsheet. They require humans to enter and cancel them or to execute. An example of such a rule might be the following:

> Buy December COMEX Gold one trading increment beyond the 5-day high.

So when the price of the December contract trades at one tick (one trading increment) beyond the highest price for gold over the last five days, the model will generate a buy order. In the case of gold, that would be $0.10, or 10¢. A trend may be underway, and new highs tell you that the market is heading higher.

That's the easy part. Back-testing around taking losses is harder. If you trade correctly, you will spend the majority of your time taking small, consistent losses more than half the time. Here's what it looks like mathematically:

Average annual rate of return: 14%

Maximum drawdown: 22%

Length of maximum drawdown: 8 months

You now have the ability to see how things "would" have looked mathematically, had you followed your rules (written today) over the last 10 years or so. What you cannot *feel* is losing money or being in a 22% drawdown that has lasted eight months. If you are managing other people's money, you are also exempt from getting phone calls from clients who are pissed at you for having lost money: "We can do this ourselves without you or your fee structure. Your results look like those we get from our asset allocator/financial advisor—what value are you adding?"

This is one reason, but not the only one, that you want to have a great deal of dry powder in self-awareness stored long before you decide to take client funds and begin managing risk. Telling yourself or your client(s) "It's not me, it's the system" is the first way to lose money or have your assets pulled. You put the trades on. You own them. Start blaming others for your failures, or your clients will doubt you. This is a mortal wound in the client–manager relationship.

"There are no external solutions to your internal problems."

If you don't take your emotional system into account, you can study all the systems and "how to" books you want, but in the end you'll know a lot about trading but not know how to trade. Most of the traders who seek me out fall into this category. They have a solid understanding of the rudiments of trading, but they can't trade effectively. Why? Hopefully, they'll get their emotional education before they spend thousands of dollars on things they don't need. Someone very wise told me, "There are no external solutions to your internal problems." If you're having a tough time trading, chances are, you don't need to learn more about the markets or commodities. You need to study yourself.

It's a complete fallacy to think that having a trading system will annul strong emotions. That's marketer-speak to induce you to believe something that you can't disprove—that is, until you own the system and you are filled with disillusion, self-doubt, and insecurity.

It's a complete fallacy to think that having a trading system will annul strong emotions.

Trading systems do not preclude meltdowns. Two members of the first group of Turtle trainees[1] had difficulty sticking to the rules they were taught. And they had Dennis and Eckhardt right next to them. One thought there had to be something more to the rules and repeatedly did not take trading signals. He was let go. The second, self-professed "best" trainee still didn't take enough of Daddy's direction and needed to get re-endowed with trading funds on more than one occasion because he thought he could add something special to the trading rules he had been taught.[2] He needed constant reloading of capital. These two students were gifted men and had two things going for them: 1) They had the other trainees in their class who were successfully using the rules each day and 2) they had two mentors at their disposal. Yet they still failed in their main task.

That's how powerful self-sabotage can be. No one is immune from the emotional hazing or the tuition that they'll have to pay. No system on the planet immunizes you from having to pay up. Having a trading system does not mean that you will follow it.

"But Mike, what about Bill Dunn?" you may say. What about him? Dunn obtained his Ph.D. in theoretical physics long before he began trading. During that time, he calibrated his emotional system with that of the scientist he was becoming. He learned to trust himself by doing lots of work in a laboratory. He failed during experiments but got back at it—that's persistence, a key trait to becoming successful at anything. Furthermore, Dunn taught physics to university-level students. He honed his expertise and learned to trust what math could explain and, as important, what it couldn't.

When you try your hand trading a system of rules, your emotional system starts flowing. If you overthink things, you'll experience a revolution inside your skull. I remember Ed Seykota telling me about a trainee he wouldn't name whose model he described as "Ready. Aim. Aim. Aim. Aim...." He was never able to pull the trigger because he overthought everything at the last minute. He couldn't live with the uncertainty of the outcome of trading, despite being on the cusp of managing risk. This is while Seykota was his mentor.

"Ready. Aim. Aim. Aim. Aim...."

Too many traders enter this world with basic knowledge of charts and try their hand at trading. That's enough to gain entry but not enough to finish. Successful trading is much harder than that. Self-aware people have a good sense of their blind spots—we all have them. With that awareness comes a sense of humility that gives a coach or mentor a lot to work with.

Besides humility, succeeding as a trader takes enormous patience. Your emotional growth may not move as quickly as you'd like it to. It may take a while for your emotional education to catch up to your level of technical knowledge. Moreover, your blind spots will evolve; they are moving targets. Your trading rules will evolve, too. It's a cycle, and your work is never going to be done.

Patience is a word that will come up a lot for a trader. It's not really a feeling itself, but a frame of mind while you are in a state of nonaction. What do you feel when you have to be patient? Do you get annoyed or anxious? Do you want to get on with it already? Is there someone in your life whom you continually have to be patient with? What does that do to your own behavior? And how do you describe your relationship with that person?

What do you feel when you have to be patient?

Imagine that person as a stock, option, foreign currency, or futures contract. I like to put myself in a state of conscious meditation when I have to be patient. I've taught myself to enjoy the moment of suspended activity. I get to rest when I have to be patient. I can meditate on the platform waiting for the 4 Train to 161st Street.

You need to have strong emotional resolve while you're busy being patient because you have to remain focused—and that takes mental energy. I find that meditation helps me control that focus for long periods of time. It's very liberating. I've taught myself that everyone on the planet can wait for me.

Where are you going, anyway, and what's the rush? In his book *Outliers*, Malcolm Gladwell suggests that it takes 10,000 hours to achieve expert status. All the time you need to spend being patient goes into those 10,000 hours, so time serves you in a positive manner. When you manage risk for a living and you have to surrender, you become more aware of "the mutations in the market that can kill you."[3]

The emotional dividend to you is that your "trading rules" appear to be validated. The risk could be that, by winning big on a mistake, you might do it again. Over time, that leads to either one of the rookie mistakes that killed the Quants' funds in the subprime morass: leverage or concentrated positions.

If your goal is to design a modeled system, how can you be compatible with something that you don't fully understand—especially when the something is yourself? You are the Black Box,[4] in that regard. The trading rules are easy once you know how they serve you. Therefore, if you don't know yourself emotionally, you are flying on autopilot—not just for the flight, but for the takeoff and landing as well.

But there's more trouble than you might imagine. Say that you drop $2,000 on a trading system and subscribe to a real-time data feed for an extra a few hundred dollars per month. You're looking at almost $10,000, and you haven't put a nickel to work in the market yet.

You run your system, and you're comfortable enough with it to create hypothetical results that you'll take to the street and begin marketing. You're all set, but you've found that the data provider you've been using, Amalgamated Data Provider, is a little expensive. You decide to switch. This happens all the time.

You link up your system to the new data feed from End of Days Data Provider and hit Run. Voilà, you get your trading output. As you compare the results of the two back tests, you find that although you kept your trading rules the same, some substantial differences between the results come out. Which do you trust, the original ones or the new ones?

So you go to your friend, who has a different trading simulator, and ask him to run your system for you. He gets two completely different results from yours using Amalgamated Data, and End of Days Data. Four back tests and four different sets of results.

Holy cow! These aren't just rounding errors. Is there a bug in the data? No, because you didn't change the data between systems. You kept the Amalgamated Data separate from the EOD Data. Good thing you spent only $3,000 between the simulation software and the data, because it could have been much more expensive. You still have another $7,000 committed, but now you have doubts.

You weren't expecting this, so you're off-center. You call customer service, but they can't tell you anything about another system that they don't sell. They tell you that you can trust your results page on their software.

The good news is that you didn't print out 50 copies of your hypothetical back-tested trading results and mail them out. It's still in PDF format—no big deal.

What do you do? Go line by line through every trade, or do you just say, "Hey, I've just done some of my very own Monte Carlo simulation, so I'm going to take the average of the four tests"?

Maybe you'll end up like the Quants, whom I discussed in Chapter 6, "Emotional Blind Spots"—Weinstein, Asness, Griffin, and Muller. I'm curious to know how they managed this phenomena using only one programming language.

> "The more you sweat in peace, the less you bleed in war." —Gen. George S. Patton

The Breakout Trader

Usually too volatile for professional money, these larger hedge funds that allocate to newer managers look to avoid large percentage-gain days move as much as they do when they face large percentage-down days. They cannot tell if you are good or lucky in that regard, so they assume that your results are random. Volatile systems are great for clients (individuals) who demand giant returns, but in my experience, these clients can't handle the drawdowns and will pull their money. They are the worst part of your trading career and have to call you every day to talk about the market. You need to cut the heat and position sizes. You also need to do some massive correlation studies along with running your system, because this "directional unit" nonsense will kill you. Do yourself a favor and seek a 12% rate of return per annum with a 4% drawdown for your first two to three years, and you'll have the large allocators lined up outside your door trying to give you money.

The emotional tradeoff is choosing between forsaking giant gains where your monthly returns can be between 50% and 100% in return for the delayed satisfaction that you get building a track record of low drawdowns and modest gains of 12% to 22% per year. The former is full of manic individuals who want you to create miracles. The latter involves professionals who run pension and endowment money. You get to choose who you want to be in business with.

Support and Resistance Trading

This is a type of trend following, but you look at the price and time chart for levels of support and resistance. You add when the price trades above the next level of resistance, and that becomes the new price where you exit your position. You trail all your positions with protective stop orders to offset your positions if the market reverses on you. You sell short when support is broken and place your protective stop above resistance.

The emotional tradeoff is a lack of envy for the breakout trader who added to his winners much sooner than you will have added to yours. The result is that he has bigger gains sooner, but he has larger and potentially more violent drawdowns because of trading size.

Moving Average Trader

Dick Donchian pioneered the moving average system. This model consists of two moving averages, a faster 5-day moving average and a slower 20-day moving average.

Moving averages (MAs) smooth out the daily chaos in a security's price. They capture the temperament of the security and define trends. In his model, when the faster 5-day MA crosses below the smoother 20-day MA, it is interpreted as generating a sell signal.

Sometimes, however, this may actually be a false signal and gets you out of an otherwise profitable trade. You have to deal with the frustration of getting out of a trade only to see it continue to make money—with you not in it.

The two moving averages are called fast or slow because of their responsiveness to each day's data. If today is volatile, it will be better reflected in the five-day moving average because there are only four other days to smooth out. Conversely, there are 19 days in the slower model to blend with today's data.

Bill Dunn of Dunn Capital and John Henry of John W. Henry are believed to trade using this system, although the specifics of how they do it may differ greatly from Donchian's original model.

This model may have a lot of false signals, chopping up equity. You can implement a filter to improve your profitability, such as using a 1- to 5-day lag before entering the trade.

With a lag, the move is well underway by the time you get a signal. It takes awhile for the daily data to become part of the moving averages, leading to aliasing a substantial portion of gains before getting a liquidating signal.

Trading the Odds

When you sit at the poker table, your odds are always changing. When you take a two-hour car trip and the GPS tells you that you should get there on time, this doesn't predict the accidents or rubber-necking miles in front of you during the trip. Your odds of arriving at the original time change with each incident.

Odds trading is probably the best of rules-based systems that automatically adjust your emotions with your behavior in real time. Instead of having a specific risk unit, odds traders are constantly adjusting their position sizes by measuring the move that they're in versus the historical ratios of such moves. They also change their tactics and the vehicles they use to manage the risk (they optimize the opportunity while keeping a strict limit on losses).

Say that the S&P 500 has had an intermediate sell-off and is down 10% over the last ten trading days. An odds trader would know that entering the market short is a bad trade at this point. Why? The average intermediate sell-off lasts about 14 trading days and is usually about 12%, so this move is just about done. By not entering short, they manage their expectations.

What they'd focus on at that point is the reversal at the bottom so that they can go long in the face of a rally. It's true, the market can be extended, but the odds trader looks for exceptional odds to skew in his favor, and he does this with position sizes.

You know the odds, so you can calculate the probabilities. If the odds are a 1:4 shot, you have a 20% chance of winning. But because you know that the move has practically exhausted itself, there is no payoff and no favorable bet size that's prudent for this trade to become positive. A short trade would be a waste of time.

This type of trading takes more time to figure out because you need to study the fundamentals of each market. If you don't like tedium, you won't like figuring out the duration and magnitude of moves for each of the markets you study. The emotional upside is that you won't be chasing your tail by getting invested in the outcome of trades that you know are suboptimal ahead of time from a reward-to-risk standpoint. However, this methodology will not help you predict the possibility of outlier events.

It's okay to be wrong, but it's not okay to stay wrong. Consistent small losses are part of the business. Admit defeat early and move on.

Chapter 8

Relative Value Trades

Everyone on the planet is a relative value trader, even when they don't trade securities or commodities. Being a relative value trader means simply choosing one product over another. You may choose Belgian waffles over English muffins, a satellite dish over cable TV, or boxers over briefs. You're bullish on the thing you choose and bearish on those things you reject. Bearish, in this case, means that you feel the goods you choose are going to provide more value.

Here's how a trade like this starts. While you're traveling in the United Kingdom, a friend recommends that you try the Best Little Belgian Waffle House in London. It hasn't been there long, but the Belgians have a thing for making the most delectable waffles and they're taking the U.K. by storm. You notice that the stock is publicly traded and has franchise opportunities. Once the rest of the world takes notice of the waffles, the stock will be in high demand. But growth won't come from Londoners. They'd have to give up their beloved crumpets to have the Belgian waffles for breakfast. Your take is that the Belgian waffles are so good that people will want to eat them all the time; hence your bullish stance. You figure that, relative to crumpets, Belgian waffles will be in higher demand over the near term. In this example, you'd be long the Belgian waffles and short crumpets.

People make these tradeoffs all the time, so I find it odd that more traders don't act in the same way. In the equity space, this is called pairs trading because you are transacting two stocks, one long and the other short. In the commodity space, it is called an intracommodity spread (long and short different months of the same commodity) or an intercommodity spread (long and short two different commodities, such as long Kansas City Wheat and short Chicago corn). The two positions are referred to as legs.

The best pairs trade I ever made in the stock market was long Microsoft (MSFT) and short Netscape (NSCP). It wasn't hard to figure out that Microsoft had leverage by having its product on more than 90% of the desktops in the world. When Microsoft decided to give away Internet Explorer (IE) embedded in its products, it was going to be hard for Netscape to compete. I profited on both legs. I think that was the only time this happened to me in 20 years of trading.

I felt that NSCP had a superior product (Navigator), but that wasn't enough to combat the fact that Microsoft had market penetration that was impossible to overcome. So the takeaway is that although I liked the NSCP product better, the smart trade was to short NSCP. This is why you cannot develop feelings for the positions in your portfolio or the securities you intend to trade. As Michael Corleone said in *The Godfather: Part III*, "Don't hate your enemies; it clouds your judgment."

One of the best pairs traders in the public eye was Julian Robertson. He was the quintessential long/short equity manager. In his meetings, if only long names were being bantered about, he'd say that his traders were not looking hard enough because he knew that there were good shorts out there, too. His guys just had to find them.

I'm not a big user of Microsoft products, but as a trader, I have to be objective because the goal is to make money, not play favorites. I don't have to be a socially responsible trader. I'm a capitalist. I have to make money, or I don't get paid.

When you attempt pairs trading, chances are, you'll have a built-in mistake: One of the two securities will probably go against you. That is an emotional concern at first, not a financial one. The same can be said if you attempt to trade option straddles or spreads, either long or short.

If I calculate that MSFT will outperform NSCP, I'm going long MSFT and short NSCP. If they both go up, I hope MSFT will go up more so that its performance will net gains that exceed the losses from my short sale on NSCP. In this situation, you want the spread to widen in your favor.

Figure 8-1 shows the spread between MSFT and NSCP prices.

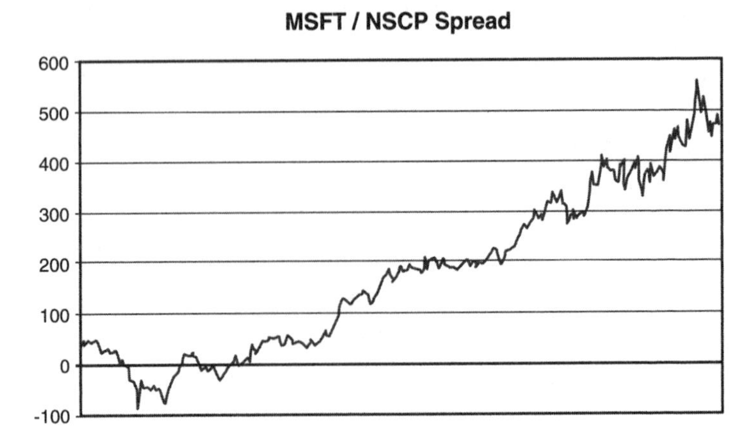

FIGURE 8-1 *This chart shows the spread between Microsoft and Netscape.*

This figure was derived from subtracting the price of NSCP from the price of MSFT. It widened after a brief sell-off early on. This spread could widen in several ways:

MSFT ↑ and NSCP ↑ less

MSFT ↑ and NSCP flat

MSFT ↑ and NSCP ↓

MSFT flat and NSCP ↓

MSFT ↓ and NSCP ↓ more

Every professional trader incorporates some form of spread trading in his or her arsenal. You don't garner the emotional rush you get with a directional trade, but you don't suffer the massive hits to your equity, either.

Equities are section based (success can be attributed to the sector of the economy), not cyclical, like commodities. Don't expect both sides of the trade to work out in your favor. You are pairing two securities that compete against one another in the same sector, hence the directional aspect of the trade. If the sector rises, you want to bet on the strongest horse in the barn and short the lamest. Relative Strength Index (RSI) is a great indicator to use for this, for both the sectors and the individual stocks.

You are hedged by trading securities in the same sector. If the market declines substantially while you have this trade on, you have a short that captures the downdraft, a tradeoff both emotional and financial.

You have a built-in mistake in your trading ethos, but because of the tradeoffs, it's an affordable one. That's the emotional key, the tradeoff. A trader who is attracted to this trade is comfortable being wrong on part of it because he knows that the stability of his account is mandated by his trade selection, his behavior, and his responsibility—what he has promised his clients. In addition, the profit from the positive side is a mechanism for controlling the loss on the negative side.

If you like to be right all the time, this trade isn't for you. Most quant funds trade pairs in some way. Pairs trading is also a low-volatility trade, so you're not likely to see your account move 10% in a week.

If you're looking for action in the market as a directional trader, you'll find it. But like a poker player who goes all in and takes a bad turn, you'll walk away from the table empty handed more times than not. I keep coming back to this because I find that when traders come to me for mentoring, their trading style is a vehicle to deliver their emotions as part of the overall motivation. Risk management does not live in this neighborhood. If you seek gains with a softer landing, look to spread trading and equity pairs trading.

Some sites on the Internet let you paper trade up to four times your capital in He-Man fashion. Do that instead. The life you save may be your own.

Some sites on the Internet let you paper trade up to four times your capital in He-Man fashion. Do that instead. The life you save may be your own.

To be a good pairs trader, you need to know how to be a short seller—and short sellers are a very different personality type than long-only traders. John Del

Vecchio who cut his teeth short selling while working for David Tice and the Prudent Bear Fund is a Chartered Financial Analyst. He reads prospectuses like most folks might read *The Girl With The Dragon Tattoo*.

"I do not believe that if you are long that you are really an owner in the business unless you own enough stock to be in control."

Del Vecchio was not born a short seller, but his personality for shorting was a perfect fit. When I asked him about his approach, he said that a trader has to be wired differently. It comes from his background as a forensics accountant, married to the instincts of a homicide detective. He explained, "I love to catch people with their hand in the cookie jar."

Del Vecchio's take is that long traders' sense of ownership is illusory: Management knows this and runs the business accordingly. "I do not believe that if you are long that you are really an owner in the business unless you own enough stock to be in control. If you were really an owner in Tyco, you wouldn't let the CEO buy a $15,000 shower curtain. But he did."[1]

After conducting hours of research before putting on a trade, Del Vecchio is not married to his positions. "I have no emotional attachment to a position," he says. "To me, a stock is just a ticker. It exists only as a way to express a trade." Being detached from a position means he is better able to manage the risk because he's not emotionally invested in the outcome of the trade.

That flies in the face of what Warren Buffett would say about owning shares of a company and equating it to ownership in the firm. But that's the art of trading. Del Vecchio has found a modus operandi, a trading methodology, that fits perfectly with his personality. That means it's easy for him to maintain discipline over long periods of time; for him, it's fun.

What's more, Del Vecchio knows my style of trading (which is largely discretionary) and some of the trades that I've put on over the last few years. "Good for you," is his take. My style is not for him, though; likewise, I have no interest in reading annual reports cover to cover.

Pairs trading is not for everyone because of the emotional concerns around short selling and unlimited downside risk. Commodities contracts of the same commodity are highly correlated, and spread traders are fine with this because they aren't looking to be right. They are looking to trade the relative value, the spread, between two contracts on the same commodity that expire in different months.

With spreads, you gain lower volatility contrasted with the individual contracts that make up the spread (legs). You can take advantage of seasonal tendencies in the production and consumption of the commodity over a year. For example, at some point, oil refineries stop creating heating oil and begin refining for gasoline. This happens after the cold season and before the summer driving season, when gas will be in higher demand and the weather will be milder. Traders have an assortment of spreads to trade to profit from the production of heating oil and gasoline based on this kind of cyclical rationale.

A similar occurrence arises in natural gas when March comes in like a lion and goes out like a lamb. Professionals trade the March/April spread in natural gas. Figure 8-2 shows the March 2011 Natural Gas contract. One of the legs to the March/April spread has been aptly nicknamed The Widowmaker, for how it's worked out for many a trader.

Source: FutureSource.com

FIGURE 8-2 *March 2010 NYMEX natural gas.*

Figure 8-2 depicts a sizable move in the March natural gas contract with trades on the NYMEX. It went from approximately $6.60 down to $4.00, or about $26,000 per contract in potential short side gains. Each $0.01 move means $100 in gains or losses for the trader in natural gas.

Figure 8-3 shows the second leg of The Widowmaker, the April contract.

Source: FutureSource.com

FIGURE 8-3 *April 2010 NYMEX natural gas.*

Figure 8-3 depicts the move in the April 2010 NYMEX natural gas contract. This one really hauled, too, moving from more than $6.00 to $4.00, representing $20,000 in price.

However, the March/April spread looked like Figure 8-4.

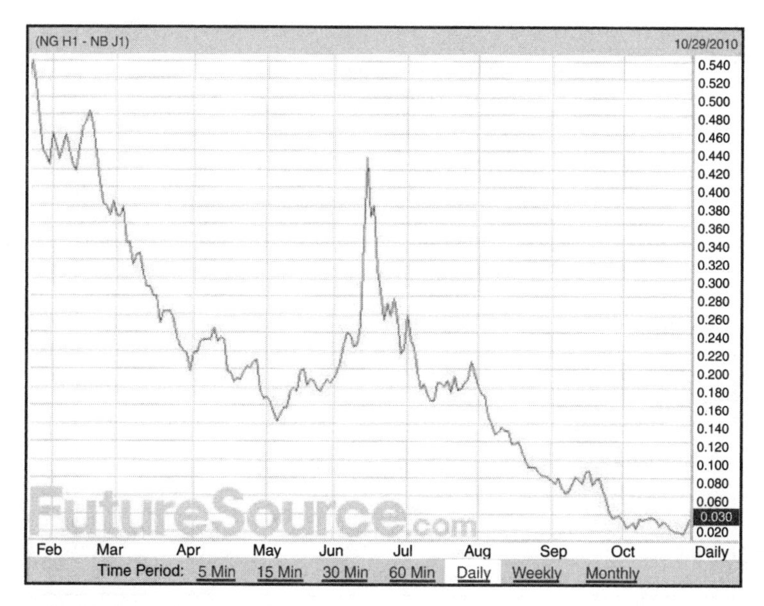

Source: FutureSource.com

FIGURE 8-4 ***The difference between the March and April 2010 natural gas contracts, a.k.a. the spread.***

The spread narrowed from a $0.52 premium in the March contract to almost equal in value with the April contract, ultimately trading to $0.035 (three and a half cents) premium to April. Traders noted that the "spread had collapsed."

Notice the volatility and the magnitude of this trade, compared to larger moves in the specific contracts: The move in the spread was profitable, yet it was approximately 25% to 20% of the downward moves in the individual contracts.

Figure 8-5 shows the seasonal tendency of this spread over the last 15 years.

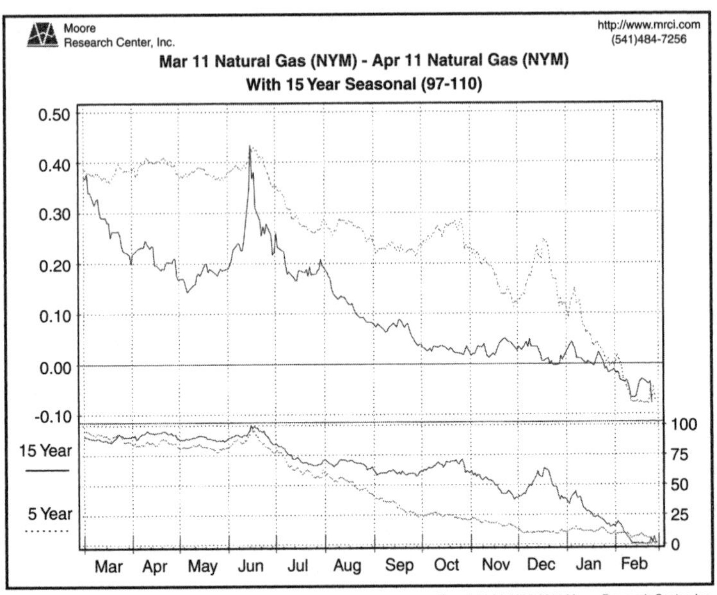

Source: Moore Research Center, Inc. Used with permission.

FIGURE 8-5 *Historical tendency for the March/April 2011 spread in natural gas.*

This spread has a seasonal tendency based on decades of cyclical supply and demand for natural gas. Spread traders and hedgers rely on the long-term value of the data. Amaranth Fund natural gas trader Brian Hunter, discussed in Chapter 6, "Emotional Blind Spots," traded against the trend and put the whole fund out of business—so you can lose. When the spread went against him, he employed what I've heard some old-timers call the "Moron Approach": He put *more on* instead of getting out with small losses. Excessive leverage was his bane as much as staying long in a spread that was narrowing.

With the trend so clear, I found it more surprising that Hunter didn't reverse the spread. Hunter was known to be a specialist in natural gas, so it's not as if he didn't understand what was going on in the natural gas market. It was a trade he'd done many times before. This final time, his emotions got the best of him and he tanked a firm because he didn't have the ability to admit he was wrong.

How you approach spreads has more to do with what you are comfortable risking. You can make money trading directional strategies on the outright contracts, or you can choose a slower and steadier approach by buying or selling spreads. All may trend, but ultimately, your choice comes down to which of the tradeoffs affect you. That's what determines how you trade. You may earn gains on one of the legs—in this case, the short March contract—but you may lose on the April, for example, because you purchased it. Spreaders are okay with this because they are trading the relationship between the contracts, not the direction of one of the legs. Their expectation is that one contract will fall (or rise) faster than the other.

This is hard for new traders to grasp because they are taught to go long on instruments that they think will go up, and go short on things that they think will go down. You can trade the spread like an investment and give it time to percolate. This involves weeks and months as a holding period, which is not typically the norm in commodities trading.

Chapter 9

The Abundance of Losses

When you begin your trading career, myriad potential outcomes are possible—some within your control and some not. In the short run, you might lose money and drop out of the market. Or you might make money but eventually lose enough to quit, get discouraged, or lose your confidence. Finally, with technical training, you may be able to trade with know-how, but eventually you will be tested in a way that leads to a massive loss, destroying your confidence and sending you to the sidelines, just like some of the traders depicted in *Market Wizards*. The trick is to figure out how to survive these early challenges to create a consistent method for *profiting* in your trading program.

Those who have lasted through bad markets, bad trades, losing periods, and bad luck seem to be the most self-aware. This chapter is about how to become more self-aware without having to spend seven years in Tibet. Many successful traders have self-awareness of a spiritual nature but are ecumenical in practice. Like me, several regularly quote from a book called *The Diamond Cutter*, by Geshe Michael Roach, which goes very well with *Market Wizards* as a companion book.

Some people trade, lose money, become demoralized, and quit. Others spend their entire life preparing technically and emotionally, and may be described in the media as amoral or unethical. But remember, just because you make a good living or are in the top 1% of wage earners does not make you "bad" or "evil."

As Roach writes, "There is a belief prevalent in America and other Western countries that being successful, making money, is somehow wrong for people who are trying to lead a spiritual[1] life."[2] Many of the largest Commodity Trading Advisors (CTAs) and hedge fund managers either run foundations or give money away each year. Many donors commit to giving funds of a specific denomination each year, so losing money in the market becomes more painful because then their charitable donations come out of their own pockets and represent a larger percentage of their overall net income.

Remember how the market works: Buyers and sellers meet each other willingly. At any moment, the market is comprised of buying and selling hedgers and buying and selling investors. They each contribute to the volume in the commodity markets, and the global auction process "discovers" the prices. In other words, no one sets the prices; they are determined by the sum total of buying and selling on the exchanges.

Many of the largest CTAs run computerized models that manage risk diligently. Traders go through layers of compliance and trading authorization. This further safeguards funds not only for traders, but also for clients of professionals. One of the main takeaways from The Diamond Cutter is that it is entirely ethical to make more than a very healthy living. But in doing so comes a responsibility to understand the genesis for your financial abundance. "As long as we do these things, making money is completely consistent with a spiritual way of life; in fact, it becomes part of a spiritual way of life."[3] The CTA firms earning hundreds of million dollars per year have done nothing but earn money for their clients consistently, with low loss drawdowns over 20 to 40 years, in some cases.

Losses bring up conflicting feelings. You need to find a way to deal with these disparate feelings, which come down to a difference between abundance and the feelings you have when you lose money. It may seem challenging to intellectualize the concept of losing with abundance, so I provide you a theory to segue.

To keep your losses small, you can place protective buy or sell stop orders on your trades. A stop is simply a price that you elect for execution as a market order. Protective buy stop orders are placed above the market to protect a short seller from a runaway market. Conversely, protective sell stop orders are entered below the market to protect you from losing more than that level in long positions in a falling market.[4] Having the stop order placed *before* all heck breaks loose protects your equity when markets move quickly and before you have a chance to place a market order. It may be too late by the time you do. Commodity traders live by their protective stop orders; so can other securities traders.

One thing Ed Seykota taught me is that a good stop order "is placed at the price where [you're] willing to transfer the risk to someone else." This is mentoring at its best, because the stop, in this context, has nothing to do with ensuring a small loss, per se. The focus is on your *willingness* to transfer the risk. You decide *willingly* where to place the stop price, and you and the new owner are equally happy to engage. You consciously decide how much to lose as a worst-case outcome. You also have an idea of how you're going to feel about losing if and when the security trades at the stop price and the order is executed. Think about that for a minute. You are responsible for all that happens from the stop placement, to the execution, and to your overall emotional constitution in managing losses and the feelings that arise with them.

> A good stop order "is placed at the price where [you're] willing to transfer the risk to someone else."

This provides traders with confidence and control. If trading profitably can be accomplished only by taking small losses (and sitting on your hands when you have profitable trades, letting your winners run), then you can feel good about taking small losses. They are part of a profitable trading scenario that all the market wizards (and other successful traders who follow them) employ. Stop orders allow you to feel relief when you get out with a minimum loss, because you end up with more money in your account for placing the stop.

Trading philosophy fits wisely with the use of stop orders. Most of the great traders I know are contrarian by nature. They don't think like everyone else, or everyone else would act like them. I think this is why journaling for a trader is invaluable. There is no other way to keep track of your thoughts and why you thought the way you did. In doing so, you'll be able to better understand how your thinking has evolved and see what over the years has servied you well and as important, what has not. For example, when you think along a contrarian line of thought, you might find yourself in the minority of that belief. In your journal you can write about the feelings you have about thinking the way you do. It's a good idea to challenge everything that you've been taught about money and finance, if only privately, in your journal.[5]

Great traders challenge their own thoughts and emotions, especially everything that they were taught in school, as a means of managing losses. On a behavioral level, I do not believe that you get ahead by conforming or getting in line. That is behavior of followers, not leaders. When you trade, you are on your own, so you become both the teacher and the student, and your journal becomes your textbook. At this point, you should begin to get comfortable with letting go emotionally of any blind faith that you've been carrying around with you. Blind faith is part of the "emotional comfort food" that I wrote about earlier.[6]

At this point, you should begin to get comfortable with letting go emotionally of any blind faith that you've been carrying around with you.

Of course, losses are perceived as problematic and negative. The important point is to exist in a profession in which losing more frequently than winning is the norm, not the exception. To begin feeling abundant, you need to break "tradition" with how your risk-management system works and add in wise management techniques, such as using stop orders. Most traders cut risk when they lose money. After losing 8% of their overall equity, they might trade based on only 70% of their remaining capital (as opposed to the 92% they actually have), to keep losses from destabilizing their larger portfolio. When you employ this tactic, you are effectively battening down the hatches. The question then becomes, "How do you cope with losses so you can continue to trade confidently and effectively?"

When you endure a trading loss, the voice you need to begin to hear is your own inner voice of encouragement, not the one that admonishes you. An overbearing parent or loved one may have inadvertently "coached" you into holding on to limiting beliefs about what you can do and accomplish in your life. That voice needs to be replaced with your inner voice that understands that when you are a professional trader, losses are part of the business. In doing so, you can unwind the wiring that mother nature has endowed you with and free yourself from becoming too defensive and turning on your creative juices to find a solution that works for your financially and emotionally.[7]

The problem is that we are our own worst enemy; we are myopic. Think of how a detective investigates a crime. If there are eight witnesses to the crime, the detective will talk to all of them. Why? If you have eight witnesses, each has his or her own version of what transpired. So my question to you is, "How do you know that your version of how things unfold in your life is the dead-center truth?" Isn't it relative to your interpretation of reality? Isn't it possible that there may be other interpretations of your actions and perceptions of you than you are aware of?

"How do you know that your version of how things unfold in your life is the dead-center truth?"

To gain a new sense of perspective about losses, take emotional inventory of your feelings. You cannot act rationally when you are still freaked out about last week's loss. As with the lesson Linda Bradford Raschke mentioned in *Market Wizards* about marking the tape in five-minute intervals, take inventory of all the things you did well compared to the ones that did not work. Focus on profitable outcomes and not so much on losses. Also write down how each of these perceived successes and failures affected you based on the actions you took. These can serve you in two ways: as entry points at your Trading Tribe or matters to learn from in future trades. If you didn't use stop losses, for example, did this lead to bigger losses? Conversely, did using stop losses reduce your loss experiences?

This is a smart exercise. If you are "too cool for school" or think you can intellectualize your feelings, then how can you expect to learn from your mistakes? I have found that the best listeners are the ones who are able to make the most progress in their trading development because in being an active listener you have to focus and be open-minded to ideas and concepts that you may disagree with or find very foreign to you at first. A person without pride—a humble person—is much better at listening to others. Such a person uses what they learn for success—for more of the green.[8]

Once you have the inventory, focus on what you did well and how you can adjust what you'd like to change. This helps in many ways unimaginable for those who do not self-reflect. This is the abundance of losses. Nothing but losses can give you this insight, but only if you are willing to listen inwardly for this insight and write it down.

Beyond the listening, you need to learn how to manage stress. Stress is a big part of trading. I don't feel stress at this point in my career because I interpret my trades with a degree of detachment. No single trade means anything, and I don't have a sense of entitlement that I am likely to win more times than I lose. However, I know from listening to my students that many suffer stress in beginning their trading careers. They are stressed to "make it" as a trader because they know that most fail.

I help them redirect that stress by focusing their energy on taking productive steps that they can control. Thinking of losses in a broader perspective improves your ability to manage them. This type of focus places you on a "crash diet" of the mind and lets you refrain from letting losses take over your analytical thought process.

Your brain is set up to respond to all types of stimuli that you consciously and unconsciously pick up through your senses. This process is control; you can allow yourself to unconsciously compute solutions to what you want to correct, even in your attitude concerning losses.

This process begins to help you work on the things that you deem important and to keep from exhausting yourself mentally from all the background noise in life that drains you, such as the stress of losing on a trade. Most of the day's stimuli that your brain interprets doesn't serve you productively. So in addition to the conscious acts of diversifying risk and placing stop orders, you can reduce stress from losses by placing them in a larger perspective.

This type of focus places you on a "crash diet" of the mind and lets you refrain from letting losses take over your analytical thought process.

As far as results are concerned, you must allow some time to "culture the pearl," as I like to say. You may get some flashes of insight immediately or none at all. But like most things worth having in life, you have to persist in your behavior if you want results. And just like trading, it is not clear when the flash of insight will arrive...sometimes in days or weeks. This may prove challenging for the student who like immediate results. Journaling the feelings that you feel when you have to be patient is a great exercise here, especially since being patient is something that will come up in many areas of our lives. The great yogis of Tibet have trusted this process for thousands of years so I think it's safe to say that you can trust the process and wait for the results.[9] This applies to trading because, truthfully, experiencing a loss can devastate your self-confidence. Learning to avoid stress and maintain a confident version of analytical thought improves your trading ability without allowing fear of loss to inhibit your approach to trading.

Within your perception of trading overall, focus on the positive outcomes and on learning more about what to do differently for the negative. Keep track of all the success that you have enjoyed. They've led you right to the spot you're in right now. You can afford 15 to 30 minutes in the morning to think these things over and get yourself into that positive mental space. You can evolve from any negative or fearful associations to one of good intentions. Take the time to envision how you'd like to be trading and the path that you think will get you there. If you keep a journal during this time, which I encourage you to do, you'll find that your trading ability and the life you're living now will converge into what you envision.[10]

From this point forward, losing money will not inhibit you or prevent you from pursing trading profits. By focusing on a few basic techniques, you find imaginative and creative ways to set the tone for your day and seek success and profit.

This approach enables you to develop your sense of self-awareness and the ability to summon all your wisdom at the precise moment necessary—your inner voice, the voice that has a wise perspective on losses as part of a larger trading strategy.

Chapter 10

Becoming an Emotional Specialist

For all the dry heaves, yoga asana, and hours of meditation I have endured, I've gotten my share of profitable trades. But there's no sense in gloating in these, because I've learned the most from the mistakes I've made.

One trading aspect that I'd like to highlight flies in the face of what you'll read in certain books and in the blogosphere. It's about becoming a specialist in one vehicle or one methodology of trading. Specialization will not come from studying books and courses on the intellectual material alone. You'll have an emotional connection with the vehicle you select and the manner in which you trade it. You're going to have a relationship with money, and the umbilical cord to it will be the leverage, frequency, and market you choose to specialize in.

With this in mind, the concept of becoming an "emotional specialist" is a requisite for accomplishing the trading philosophy I suggest. An emotional specialist has these attributes:

- Approaches trading with an awareness of the role of emotions, beyond the more logical timing and risk management aspects of trading.
- Accepts loss as a fact of life and as part of the mix between profit and loss, recognizing that losses occur for good reasons and that the key to trading success is *managing* the degree of loss.
- Recognizes that control over profitability rests with the emotional makeup of each and every trader, a fact equally significant with the technical skills of product selection.

- Knows that the human brain reacts to all input, but most of all to the input an individual creates for him- or herself. Writing down the input that an individual wants to operate on is a method for creating the desired path to profitability.

In *The New Market Wizards,*[1] Linda Raschke recommends that each new trader study a market by following it in five-minute intervals to get to know it well. I followed up with her about this advice during an interview for this book. "The benefits of taking periodic readings serve several purposes," she says. "When you write something down, it works a different part of the brain than when you just sit passively."[2] This makes a lot of sense because humans learn in three ways: reading, listening, and writing.

Raschke's analysis has another aspect that helps build your inner voice. "Writing things down recenters you in the present, and it will enhance your concentration," she says. Yes, writing in these time increments will enhance your concentration because you must focus. Monks meditate frequently each day because practice makes perfect. The mind is a beast, and you know this if you've ever had to sit quietly and not think about anything. You need to practice your meditation to get better at it. You can't do it once and say, "It's not for me." You're missing the point. Meditation helps build your concentration and focus. "Ultimately," Raschke says, "it will help you stay in control of yourself."[3]

"Writing things down recenters you in the present, and it will enhance your concentration."

The meditative quality of self-awareness is an essential attribute for the emotional specialist. It provides you with a control mechanism. When you experience unexpected loss, you know that gut feeling of losing control. Meditation helps you maintain balance and understand both why losses are occurring and, most important, how you can control losses in the future. To better understand how meditation works, think of it as a look from without to within, instead of the other way around. Meditation helps you not only understand loss, but also manage profit and loss in the future *and* manage the emotions you experience when losses arise.

Think of the experience of loss in relation to what Raschke says about the ways we learn. You might think of meditation as just something you undertake as part of reading the electronic ticker tape,[4] but there's more to her method. "I use tape reading to see volume swells to find something out of the ordinary," she says. "I have several 4×4 squares of prices and the net change of the major groups on my monitor. I have a sense of when something is going to happen, and I am looking for the confirmations on the large-volume movements on the trends to the upside [that] now is the time to add to my positions. I'm looking for the confirmation in the related commodities for strong money flows."[5]

> Question: "How do you think Raschke has this feel for the markets?"
>
> Answer: "By having developed tremendous focus and sense of concentration."

The five-minute exercise has very little to do with the market itself, but everything to do with you.

Raschke trades commodities, and she was referring to them in her explanation. But you can apply this exercise to any asset class and use it to your advantage.

When you become a specialist, you are coordinating your emotions with the vehicles you trade, leverage, and trading frequency. If you can figure out how all these components feel to you, you can easily determine your style of trading and the type of trading that works best. This is essential to succeeding as an emotional specialist.

After awhile, you might begin to appreciate one of the major tenets of this book: The vehicles that you trade and the manner in which you trade them are nothing more than an emotion-delivery system. You pick the security and the way to trade to get that the feelings you want or to avoid others that you don't want.

Table 10-1 shows the matrix for an equity trading-based emotional-delivery system.

TABLE 10-1 *Matrix for an Equity Trading-Based Emotional-Delivery System*

Leverage	Holding Period	Country	Market Bias
1:1	HFT	United States	Long
2:1	Intraday	Foreign	Short
4:1	1–3 days		Pairs (both)
6.7:1			
10:1			

The order of these variables does not matter, so you can mix and match them to get 90 mathematical combinations of feelings that you can (and want to) obtain.

You can benchmark all these with one denominator, the emotional value of financial loss, to get closer to the manner of trading that suits you best. In other words, you can delete some of the combinations in which you don't like the feelings they give you. That's a good thing. This also is another component of becoming an emotional specialist, controlling the trade configuration that works for you on that emotional level.

Although you can trade without the help of a coach, mentor, spiritual guru, or Tribe Chief,[7] your long-term success without help relies on luck. Rarely does someone have the emotional constitution to make it as a trader right from the start. I was lucky to understand early on that successfully navigating my "salad days" in trading had more to do with my keeping losses small than with making gains.

> The past two trading sessions had been a gift and my main goal always was to protect my equity.

A full 17 years after my bout with the Shaman Pharmaceutical trade that I wrote about in Chapter 3, "My Tuition," I can still feel the burn in my throat from that emotional night of having to deal with the uncertainty until the next day's session. All of what I learned from my errors then paid off. A particular managed account started with $100,000, and by the time I was done buying sugar, we had about 35 contracts in the account. At about $2,000 of margin per contract, I had about $70,000 posted on margin, but the contract had gone from 9 to 21 over the same period. I kept buying all the way up, while moving my protective sell stop higher each time. (Notice I don't call it a "stop-loss order." Because I was making money, it was more of a "stop–give back order." Losing money from the prior day's balance just means that you don't make as much, but you're still making money. I say this because I'm always looking for bias in the markets and in the language we use around trading.)

I bought early on between 6 and 9 and stopped buying at around 14 or 15, but it seemed that each day it went higher. Then, in a rare gift from the universe, the market went parabolic over the course of the last three to four days. It jumped from 18 to 19.25. The next day, the shorts must have been bleeding out of their eyes because, at the open, the contract jumped again, rising over 1.00 to a high over 21.

I called my execution trader and put in a stop at 21.00 for the whole boat. I knew better than to put a protective sell stop for all my contracts at such a round number, but the past two trading sessions had been a gift and my main goal always was to protect my equity.

I had learned from the Michael Marcus chapter in *Market Wizards* that I wasn't going to miss a big move in any one market. I knew from reading the instructions George Soros imparted to Stan Druckenmiller that when the fundamentals and technicals are in alignment, you can't have enough of a position on.[8] And most importantly, I had learned from my own mistakes over the years that protecting my equity at all times is the first order of business.

When the fundamentals and technicals are in alignment, you can't have enough of a position on.

Protecting my equity at all times is the first order of business.

I remember feeling calm and controlled: I had the right methodology and I wasn't going to try to figure out when the top for sugar was in. I added to my winners well beyond what any system would dictate—this was a discretionary trade. I trailed with a liquidating sell stop order that would have taken me out of the entire position. I calculated the stop price and calibrated it for both financial gain and emotional satisfaction. I respected the market and the fact that probably hundreds of traders knew sugar trading much better that I did. I knew I was lucky because I hadn't gotten knocked out of the trade, although there was ample volatility. I was grateful for the learning experience, but I was also hypervigilant in making sure that my trader had the protective sell stops in each day.

This trade was made available to me only because I was self-aware—that was the only part I could control. Persistence and determination come from being self-aware. And sugar tripling in price was just dumb, random luck. We are powerless over the markets.

> Truth: I never would have guessed that sugar would be the trade of the year.
>
> Truth: I never would have guessed that I would have kept adding to my position between 6 and 15.
>
> Truth: I never would have guessed then that today's price for sugar is 50% higher than where I liquidated the position years ago.

What I did have going for me were several qualities that Dickson G. Watts delineated in *Speculation As a Fine Art*:

- Self-reliance
- Judgment
- Courage
- Prudence

Sugar tripling in price was just dumb, random luck. We are powerless over the markets.

None is a technical indicator; all are personal characteristics. This means that emotional control (as an attribute of the emotional specialist) is ultimately much more significant than technical insight. The ability to track chart patterns and skillfully time trades is widely respected and emulated—until the expert loses everything in one ill-timed trade. What does that do emotionally? In this occurrence (which is not at all unusual), self-reliance was a flaw, judgment was in error, courage was fool's courage, and prudence was *ignored.* Thus, the emotional specialist needs not only to apply these four attributes as priorities in trading timing and decision making, but also to remain pliable in how these are applied. This fifth attribute, pliability, is far beyond the humility you may associate with prudence. A prudent trader may simply be conservative by avoiding excessive risk. A pliable trader recognizes the flaws in any set of skills, including emotional ones. You may be deceived through excessive application of self-reliance, judgment, courage, and prudence, just as you may be misled by chart-reversal signals or volume spikes. Dickson G. Watts, a founding member of the New York Cotton Exchange and its president from 1878 to 1880, certainly knew this from his own experiences in the market. "There is no royal road to success in speculation," he said. "We do not undertake, and it would be worse than folly to undertake, to show how money can be made. Those who make for themselves or others an infallible plan delude themselves and others."[9]

By arming yourself with knowledge on emotional as well as technical levels, which takes a long time, you will be able to better interpret market action. When you master the entire package, you will be able to trade any market better. You simply need to do one thing very well, and you'll have a great career. Part of the ethos at SAC Capital Advisors, the eponymous trading firm founded by Steve Cohen, was to have traders focus on one sector so that they were not trading everything from Yahoo! (tech) to Exxon (energy) to Pfizer (pharma). If they traded tech, they stuck with tech. If they traded energies, they stuck with energies. Their knowledge was narrowly focused, but it ran deep.

This served two purposes. First, traders were less likely to be caught off guard, because they were experts in the sector. Second, they were not chasing their tails trying to figure out what was happening with many companies within many sectors. Cohen required self-awareness in his traders by limiting the securities he allowed them to trade. He built self-awareness into his risk-management system.[10]

You don't need to run a mechanized mathematical system to be a successful trader. That flies in the face of many things I have explained, but it's the truth. The world of trading is a lot larger than computers and systematized rules. You can expand Table 10-1 to include all the variables of your own system. Your system can provide you with many more feelings than what you have come to expect. You want to study the variance between trading behavior signals that your system generates (or does not).

When you figure out who you are emotionally, deciding on the vehicle, the degree of leverage, and the frequency of trading will be easy.

If you learn what feelings you like and don't like, you'll be far ahead of your competition. But you have to start with your feelings and emotions, not a "how to" book on trading. When you figure out who you are emotionally, deciding on the vehicle, the degree of leverage, and the frequency of trading will be easy. You will have converted yourself into an emotional specialist, and then the decisions you have to make every day will be clearer because you'll know not only how and when to trade, but also why.

Chapter 11

Listen to Your Inner Voice

"But darkness makes me fumble
For a key to a door that's wide open."

—Stewart Copeland, "*Darkness*," from the album *Ghost in the Machine*

As a trader, improving your ability to listen improves your trading dramatically—listening to *why* someone is speaking the words, and the manner in which they are speaking, not just the literal meaning. When you listen this way, you open your mind to the true meaning of what is being conveyed. This includes listening to your own inner voice.

Not just the information alone matters—so does the emotion behind it, the motivation of the person speaking. The speaker (analyst, trader, portfolio manager, central banker) may be unaware of what he or she is communicating also because that person is not aware of his or her inner voice. People act on their emotions but speak literally about intellectual things—especially men.

Indian philosopher and mystic Jiddu Krishnamurti said, "When you are listening to somebody, completely, attentively, then you are listening not only to the words, but also to the feeling of what is being conveyed, to the whole of it, not part of it."[1]

To listen in this manner, you need to focus intensely. A few years ago, the National Science Foundation did a study that suggested that people can have as many as 60,000 thoughts per day. This is before you tune in to the TV and social media. You can imagine how exhausting this must be from a "physical noise" standpoint. Most of these are innocuous thoughts and don't serve you in any way. But each takes up energy and brainpower. And when you consume brainpower, you tire mentally and physically as time transpires. So, the very thing that you think is supposed to help you is actually draining you of your valuable energy.

On top of this, your nervous system picks up on stimuli and triggers thoughts and ideas. If you're on the trading floor or at home, chances are, you'll have at least one TV near you emitting sound. You may have several TVs on, with various channels all making noise. Furthermore, each channel now has to junk up the screen with "breaking news" headlines (the scroll), as well as updated quote boards and charts of the securities the guests are talking about. I'm exhausted just writing this.

All this information is statistical noise, banal data points. Supergorgeous women with high-tech backdrops announce the news with authoritative voices that communicate to you that it must be important and *urgent*. If you're not up-to-date, you're out of touch. That may be true, but it has no effect on your profit and loss (P&L) statement.

Breaking news: Lindsay Lohan to drop last name, Dow off 119.

Most of the flashing screens, charts, scrolling ticker tape, and headlines loaded with a phenomenon known as causality ("Breaking news: Lindsay Lohan to drop last name, Dow off 119") is all there to entertain you. This is the definition of *infotainment*.

I haven't had pay TV for four years now. As you can imagine, I don't miss this at all. The whole process is engineered to mesmerize you into thinking that you can't live without it. But you can—and, frankly, you *must* if you want to get control of what Buddhists and meditation gurus call *monkey mind*,[2] a string of thoughts that swing like a monkey from tree to tree. A person suffering from monkey mind cannot be present and seems addicted to the flow of data, of which value points are passing and fleeting.

If you look closely at your behavior, you may start thinking that your professional process is actually a ritual that you have set up to consume your brainpower before you've put a single trade on. But it feels good, and that's the point. This is where your inner voice can act as a controller to keep you on course.

Understanding data from any source is part of learning, but if you don't know yourself, it doesn't matter what you know, where you learn it from, or how frequently you get your data. Familiarity will begin to make you numb. Your inner voice should question all of it continuously, asking, "Is this relevant, important, or essential to what I need to know at the moment?" This is a new way of listening, not only to others, but to yourself as well.

Your professional process is actually a ritual that you have set up to consume your brainpower before you've put a single trade on.

Part of learning to listen in a new way involves becoming a contrarian and thinking 180 degrees out of phase with everyone else. Education is important, but it is more important to learn to listen to yourself. Your inner voice is the single most important tool that you have at your disposal. However, to be good at this, you have to learn to trust yourself.

A meditation group, yoga practice, a solitary quiet endeavor, or a Trading Tribe can be invaluable in this regard. If you are forced to listen (or hear noise), you will be easily distracted and find it nearly impossible to quiet your mind. Months or years later, you will learn to let it go and "just be there," as my friend and teacher Erich Schiffmann says.

Schiffmann is my life-long yoga teacher, meditation coach, and friend. He doesn't trade, to my knowledge, but he's had a profound effect on helping me develop my consciousness and self-awareness. "The smarter you get, the more you realize how little you know," he says. "The more you realize how little you know, the less willing you are to only use that information. Once you realize that there is an Internet of the mind, then you can begin to get online with it. The smartest thing to do is to do everything you can in order to get online, so to speak."[3] This recalls something Schiffmann wrote in his great book *Moving into Stillness*: Whenever you have to make a very important decision, stop for ten minutes and "take a beat"—sit quietly and ask the universe for guidance. Ask "Where can this go wrong?" or "What am I not taking into consideration?" Time is always on your side, and this practice of listening to your inner voice requires that quiet time.

> "The smarter you get, the more you realize how little you know. The more you realize how little you know, the less willing you are to only use that information."

Making decisions by yourself doesn't make sense, especially when managing risk and trading where the unknowns are immeasurable. "Instead of making up your mind yourself with the little information you have in your little hard drive, do your best to throw the question out to the universe, to the best of your ability—'silent-mind' it so the download can begin from the universe," Schiffmann advises.[4]

The book *Talent Is Overrated*, by Geoff Colvin, got me thinking. In the trading world, education is overrated. People with average IQs financially outperform those with high IQs a whopping 70% of the time,[5] and a study on this topic concluded that only 36% of those tested[6] were able to identify their emotions in real time with any accuracy. Two-thirds of people are controlled by emotions that they cannot identify. This has huge implications for traders and what they need to do to become better traders. You need to have a system for finding out what your feelings are trying to tell you—especially your subconscious feelings. These feelings are always running in the background in everything you do, although you are unaware of them. You probably can see the results of this subconscious system but are likely not to know the progenitors.

Market wizard Linda Bradford Raschke also has a lot to say to traders. "New traders have too much to think about and too many decisions. ...Strive...to free yourself from the chatter. The more you can preset the course of action, the more you can alleviate stress. Too many variables each occurring at the same time will give you too much stress."[7] Here's another market wizard telling you to cut the stress out of your life so you can make better decisions.

Raschke says about stress, "Keep it in check, because a little stress will be good for performance, but too much will shut you down. Stay at an emotional even keel. Experience is one thing, but if your mental health and spiritual side is out of kilter, that is going to affect your sense of concentration. Experience won't matter."[8]

If you don't learn about your feelings, your outcome is predicted whether you know it or not. You might as well surrender and learn about your feelings so that you can have a more profound effect in the navigation of your trading career.

With two-thirds of the crowd being controlled by emotions they can't identify, you can define part of your trading edge immediately by developing your sense of self-awareness. This turns the odds in your favor: By trading against you, your opponents are, in effect, a "1-2 shot"—and you don't even know what the acronym MACD[9] stands for. You are the favorite with a large edge, and you might not know how to trade yet.

> When you meditate, you gain self-knowledge. If I'm wrong, that flies in the face of 4,000 years of history that predate Buddhism and go back before 1,800 B.C. When you understand yourself better, you begin to understand the market better and you're not drawn into as many suboptimal trades. The key for traders is to live for another day. You become a superior trader when you evolve to know that it's a game of playing the best defense among your peers instead of being a prescient stock picker or commodities picker.

Question: "Don't professional commodities traders like you *love* risk?"

Answer: "I love risk like a fireman loves fire, which means I do not love risk. I'm just able to deal with risk better when I rely on my inner voice."

Aaron Brown, chief risk manager at trading firm AQR Capital,[10] says at one point in his career when focused on his own trading. "I didn't have that edge to care about trading after a certain point," he says. "I didn't lose touch, and I still like making money, but I lost the edge that I think you need. I became more academic in the roles that I play now. I stay grounded that way. Once you lose the laser focus, you should not try to manage risk. The worst thing that can happen is that you can make it back tomorrow. The real difference between the amateurs and professional poker players is that, after playing for 72 hours straight, professionals really care about the $500 in the pot. If you don't have that, you're not going to win long term. Unless you really care for every position, you're not going to make it as a trader."[11]

I love risk like a fireman loves fire; I'm just able to deal with risk better.

Paul Tudor Jones made a candid remark after a particularly tough day of trading when he took a 5% loss. He stated that it was not about the money, but the fact that he had been so completely wrong in his analysis. What I think makes Jones the best is that, although he had been hit emotionally and intellectually, he did not get derailed. He acknowledged his shortcoming in a moment of humility. He also acknowledged that such days occur many times over a trader's career. This happened during a period in his career when he doubled his accounts many years in a row. When I meet new traders who cannot act with candor or humility, I get a sense that they are not going to be long for the business. Why? Because they not only don't listen to their inner voice, but seem to not even know it is there.

Commodity Trading Advisor (CTA) David Harding explained how his firm, Winton Capital, achieved success: "We analyze massive volumes of noisy data from the markets, trying to find patterns that we can 'bet' on. I would say we have considerable humility compared with most participants in the financial markets, who create elaborate stories. We know that we know almost nothing, but the 'almost nothing' we know isn't completely nothing, and we only bet on that. It's a bit like a scientific experiment, because quite often we fail. But overall we make more money than we lose."[12]

Travis Bradberry and Jean Greaves of TalentSmart, a firm specializing in training people to increase their emotional quotient (EQ), found that 90% of top performers in the workforce are also card-carrying members of the emotionally intelligent, an attribute of those who heed their inner voice. The two also found that they earned an average of $29,000 more per year than folks with lower EQs.[13] The addition of $29,000 per year might not mean much to you—that's subjective. They concluded that each point increase in EQ meant another $1,300 in annual salary.

This all means that you can control losses, to some degree. Excessive use of leverage can exacerbate an otherwise small move. Having fewer shares or a smaller number of contracts in your account can annul the effect of large price swings in a security. It is a matter of

> Your emotions and feelings are your master as they control your behavior.

maintaining focus during trades that are losing, and making that just as easy as it is to keep your focus when your trade is winning.

When you choose to trade Forex with 50:1 leverage, the financial goals exist only on the surface. The real goals are churning away inside your skull, an internal debate in your inner voice. Surrender to those feelings and learn from them, because they aren't going away. Your emotions and feelings are your master as they control your behavior. They take you on a long ride until you finally get what they are trying to teach you. Technical trading skills alone will get you only so far. You'll also get hung up in your decision-making process by listening to too many analysts and other managers. Anyone you see or hear on TV has an agenda. There's no guarantee that what experts or you perceive as an undervalued security will rise, nor that an overvalued security will fall. If you had a trading rule that stipulated not buying stocks with a P/E (price-to-earnings) ratios[14] of greater than 20, you would have missed some good opportunities. Even Warren Buffett missed Microsoft and Apple, which had high P/E ratios. It's arrogant to think that you are on to something and that "the rest of the world will catch up" to your thinking. The markets determine the value of a stock or commodity; value isn't based on what an analyst says something is worth. If you can surrender to the fact that price tells you everything you need to know, you can forfeit your ego and let the natural flow of things take over, both in your head and in the markets.

You can learn a lot about your feelings by studying price. When you become too emotionally attached to the entry price, you are going to kill your opportunities and your equity, too. Let go of how exact you have to be with your entry. As in real estate, you make your money when you get out: selling to keep your losses small and selling via a trailing stop to make sure you don't give back all your gains.

> It's arrogant to think that you are on to something and that "the rest of the world will catch up" to your thinking. The markets determine the value of a stock or commodity; value isn't based on what an analyst says something is worth.

Here's another way you can learn about yourself. Say that you make a big gain from a trade. What do you immediately feel after the trade and in the 24-hour period following? You are likely to feel euphoric, proud, smart, and brave. What do you do? Do you get up and tell everyone? Do you mention it on Twitter or text message your significant other? What feeling follows the feeling of locking in large gains? Who did you call or contact? What response are you looking for? Intentions equal results, and if you've begun with the end in mind, texting your girlfriend about your awesomeness might be the goal. Getting emotional feedback from your parents might be the goal. In the end, the money might be irrelevant.

But if the market goes against you significantly and you don't have a predetermined exit strategy, you will likely feel despairing or despondent. This is the other side of the emotional coin that you must deal with. If you don't like it or can't deal with it, you must decide on a new "system" or set of rules—or, more importantly, better risk management based upon the tradeoffs you're willing to make. Your inner voice needs to decide on the dialogue as well as on the platform. You get to choose both, but as you've already read, sometimes they don't come easy. Accessing your inner voice comes with quieting your mind. Why is this so important? Follow my logic: Meditation can be defined as a process of quieting your mind through breathing techniques. Your mind controls your overall attitude. Your attitude affects your behavior and your persistent behavior predicts where you end up in life.

There's no overall correct answer for the world of traders; there's only the correct answer for you.

There's no overall correct answer for the world of traders; there's only the correct answer for you. If you like the idea of trying to grow your trading account, you must also embrace the feeling of the potential downside that goes with it. They are perfect emotional complements, and you cannot take one without the other.

The traders interviewed and discussed in this book are intelligent, cunning, and pioneering. Each has a different style of trading. Each trades a methodology that needed to evolve or converge with the trader's ever-evolving sense of emotional intelligence, level of consciousness, and sense of self-awareness. Each has a direct connection to his or her inner voice.

Endnotes

Chapter 1

1. Jason Zweig, *Your Money & Your Brain: How the New Science of Neuroeconomics Can Help Make You Rich* (New York: Simon & Schuster, 2007).

Chapter 2

1. A Trading Tribe is an association of like-minded individuals who commit to excellence, personal growth, and supporting and receiving support from each other. Trading Tribe is a trademark owned by Ed Seykota. More can be found at www.tradingtribe.com.

2. Jonah Lehrer, *How We Decide* (Boston: Houghton Mifflin Harcourt, 2009).

Chapter 4

1. Jack Schwager, *Market Wizards* (New York: Harper Business, 1993), p. 23.

2. In this case, the expression "bid limit" means that the bid price would have risen to its daily maximum and soybean trading would be halted on the Chicago Board of Trade (CBOT). Then no one would be able to buy more soybeans.

3. Schwager, p. 23–24.

4. You can hear Bill Dunn speak about emotions and trading in a two-part video interview I did with him in Los Angeles.

5. For the record, Dunn did make one discretionary trade, per se, but it was more of a portfolio reallocation. He offset all his commodity positions and put his clients' assets at 100% cash just before December 31, 1999, during the Y2K hoax. He did so to protect his clients' funds from this unfounded computer phenomenon. Nothing happened, though, and it ended up costing Dunn several percentage points in performance.
6. Ed Seykota, *The Trading Tribe* (Incline Village: Ed Seykota, 2005), p. 118.
7. Mike Covel, *Trend Following* (New York: FT Press, 2005), p. 64.
8. Yoda, from "Star Wars VI: Return of the Jedi." "Luke, do not underestimate the powers of the Emperor, or suffer your father's fate you will." In other words, make your feelings your ally or else you'll be like every other trader who gets derailed emotionally.

Chapter 5

1. Jack Schwager, *New Market Wizards* (New York: Harper Business, 1992).
2. Interview with Peter Borish, September 2010.
3. Ibid.
4. Ibid.

Chapter 7

1. This is a group of trader trainees taught by Richard Dennis and William Eckhardt.
2. According to BarclayHedge CTA, there is only one Turtle whose trading results do not exist.
3. Victor Sperandeo, "To The Victor," Trader Monthly Hall of Fame article.
4. The term "black box" is a slang expression for computerized trading systems. It is not to be confused with high-frequency trading, though.

Chapter 8

1. Interview with the author, March 2011.

Chapter 9

1. "Spiritual" in this regard does not mean "belief in a supreme being." These days, it signifies that people believe that they are part of something much bigger than themselves.
2. Geshe Michael Roach, *The Diamond Cutter: The Buddha on Managing Your Business and Your Life,* Kindle Edition (Doubleday Religion, 2009).
3. Ibid.
4. Stop orders can be used to enter the market long or short also. However, execution is generated when the security reaches that price. At execution, the price may have moved farther.

5. Roach, 2009.
6. *Ibid.*
7. *Ibid.*
8. *Ibid.*
9. *Ibid.*
10. *Ibid.*

Chapter 10

1. Jack Schwager, *The New Market Wizards* (New York: Harper Business, 1992).
2. Interview with the author, October 2010.
3. *Ibid.*
4. Reading the ticker tape is a technique used by many traders such as Ace Greenberg. Traders choose a price reference point by watching prices on the tape and trade in the direction of the movement away from that reference point.
5. Interview with the author, October 2010.
6. Depending on your account size and your broker/dealer, a trader is afforded various degrees of leverage. Accounts under $25,000 can get 2:1 leverage. Above $25,000 is 4:1 leverage, and above $100,000 is 6.7 to 1.
7. Trading Tribe, Chiefdom, and other similar terms are Trademarks owned by Ed Seykota.

8. Sebastian Mallaby, *More Money Than God* (New York: Penguin, 2010).

9. Dickson G. Watts, *Speculation as a Fine Art and Thoughts on Life* (New York: Traders Press, 1965).

10. "How SAC Thrives on the Genius of Clutch," at MartinKronicle.com.

Chapter 11

1. *You Are the World,* Talks at the University of California, Berkeley, 1969.

2. https://secure.wikimedia.org/wikipedia/en/wiki/Mind_monkey.

3. Erich Schiffmann. Interview with the author, September 2010.

4. *Ibid.*

5. Emotional Intelligence 2.0, Bradberry and Greaves.

6. *Ibid.*

7. Linda Bradford Raschke. Interview with the author, 2011.

8. *Ibid.*

9. MACD stands for moving average convergence divergence.

10. AQR stands for applied quantitative research.

11. Interview with the author, March 2011.

12. NewScientist Opinion, at www.newscientist.com/article/mg20827895.000-hedgefund-philanthropist-physics-can-save-the-planet.html.
13. For the definition of P/E ratio, see www.investopedia.com/terms/p/price-earningsratio.asp.

INDEX

E

F

G–H

I–J–K

L

FT Press
FINANCIAL TIMES